'This book has renewed in m[...]nore, and to delight in his favour.'
Lyndon Bowring, Chair and [...]

'*Jesus, Lover of My Soul* is a de[...], heartwarming and inspiring guide to deeper spiritual intimacy with God. It reorientates our desires – whether met, half met or unmet – to their true and ultimate fulfilment. But it's so much more than a call to pursue Christ; it's an invitation to feel *his* desire for us. The result is a real tonic for the soul.'
Tim Chester, faculty member of Crosslands Training and author of *You Can Change: God's transforming power for our sinful behaviour and negative emotions* and *Enjoying God: Experience the power and love of God in everyday life*

'Throughout the centuries, generations of Christians have borne witness to the Song of Songs as the means by which they experience deepest intimacy with Christ, their heavenly Bridegroom. This series of devotional reflections will help Christians today to share in that same passionate experience, to revel in Jesus' love, to know the joy of his delight in us and to long desperately for his return when he will sweep us up into his eternal embrace. I really liked the book – both the idea and the execution – and I hope it will open up the Song of Songs to lots of people in a deeper way.'
Ros Clarke, Associate Director of Church Society, and writing a commentary on the Song of Songs

'One of the most significant cultural drivers of our age is the search for intimacy and the hunger to eliminate alienation. We need an antidote to the misplaced enthronement of sex as the ultimate quest for intimacy. The Song of Songs is one of the "lost" books of the Bible in the devotional life of Christians as well as the preaching of evangelical churches. *Jesus, Lover of My Soul* was created on the anvil of sermons preached in a local church. Each chapter bears witness to what Karl Barth termed the "unquenchable yearning" in the Song of Songs.'
David Coffey OBE, Past President of the Baptist World Alliance

'Julian Hardyman offers us here a brilliant explanation of the sometimes confusing Song of Songs. But there is more than just expertise in this book. It is a powerful and much needed reminder to Christians that Christ desires us and wants us to respond to that desire.'
Dr Simon Gathercole, Professor of New Testament Studies, Faculty of Divinity, University of Cambridge; Director of Studies in Theology and Fellow of Fitzwilliam College, Cambridge

'What a remarkable book! Julian Hardyman was once my student, but more recently he has, on several occasions, served as a wise pastor for me personally. I was surprised to find myself convinced by his argument that the Song of Songs can be read not only as a beautiful description of human romantic love but also as a divinely inspired guide that can draw believers into a closer personal relationship with Christ. It has certainly done that for me.'
Dr Wayne Grudem, Distinguished Research Professor of Theology and Biblical Studies, Phoenix Seminary, Arizona

'I am constantly challenged by our desire to know God better, to "see his face" and experience him more. *Jesus, Lover of My Soul* is a timely reminder of the amazing truth that we don't just desire him, but Christ desires us! As Julian explores the imagery of Christ, and his bride, the church, we are energized by the truth that "we stand complete in him".'
Nola Leach, Chief Executive Officer, CARE, UK

'A remarkable combination of intellect, imagination and devotion. Thoroughly contemporary, engaging with our culture as well as the biblical revelation. Often Julian allows us to go quite deeply into his own soul, and so reaches deeply into ours.'
Peter Lewis, Minister at Cornerstone Church, Nottingham, for many years

'This book does many things. It makes the Song of Songs accessible. It takes the text seriously. It engages with both Puritans and contemporary culture. But what *Jesus, Lover of My Soul* does best of all

is give us a grown-up view of a passionate and intimate relationship with Christ. As such, this is a rare and precious gift to the church. Read it and you will know more of the passion that Christ feels for you.'
Steve Midgley, Senior Minister at Christ Church Cambridge and Executive Director of Biblical Counselling UK

'Preaching and writing on the Song of Songs is always a courageous thing to do – especially when challenging interpretative assumptions that have become well established in recent years. We all owe Julian Hardyman a huge debt for having the courage to do just that in this brilliant book. Like the great Song of Songs itself, this book is at times unsettling and even shocking, yet full of insight and practical help. It is perhaps the most helpful thing I have ever read on how to cultivate a deep and satisfying intimacy with Christ.'
John Risbridger, Minister and Team Leader, Above Bar Church, Southampton

'This is an extraordinary book. An extended analysis of the Song of Songs, it speaks into the very depths of our own desire for intimacy and love, but then lifts that desire into the spiritual heights that the Song reaches. The book is personal, honest and transparent, yet it is also scholarly, sharing nuggets from a host of other insightful authors in a way that speaks so relevantly into our culture today. The text focuses carefully on the Song itself, but draws on so much biblical literature that we soon realize its central theme is everywhere, and inexhaustible. Please read this book and indulge yourself in intimacy; you will soon find you are bathing in the warmth and fullness of the love of God.'
Dr Elaine Storkey, member of the General Synod of the Church of England, President of Tearfund, broadcaster and author

JESUS, LOVER OF MY SOUL

Julian Hardyman was converted to Christ as a teenager. He studied English at university, and worked in printing and publishing before training for pastoral ministry at Cornerstone Evangelical Church, Nottingham, and at Trinity Evangelical Divinity School, Deerfield, Illinois, USA. He has been Pastor at Eden Baptist Church, Cambridge, since 1996. Julian is the author of *Maximum Life* and *Idols* (both IVP), and of *The Joy of Service* and *Fresh Pathways in Prayer* (10ofthose).

JESUS, LOVER OF MY SOUL

FRESH PATHWAYS TO SPIRITUAL PASSION

JULIAN HARDYMAN

INTER-VARSITY PRESS
36 Causton Street, London SW1P 4ST, England
Email: ivp@ivpbooks.com
Website: www.ivpbooks.com

First published in 2020

British Library Cataloguing-in-Publication Data
A catalogue record for this book is available from the British Library.

ISBN: 978-1-78974-173-5
eBook ISBN: 978-1-78974-174-2

10 9 8 7 6 5 4 3 2 1

Set in 11/14pt Minion Pro
Typeset in Great Britain by CRB Associates, Potterhanworth, Lincolnshire
Printed in Great Britain by Ashford Colour Press Ltd, Gosport, Hampshire

Produced on paper from sustainable forests.

Inter-Varsity Press publishes Christian books that are true to the Bible and that communicate
the gospel, develop discipleship and strengthen the church for its mission in the world.

IVP originated within the Inter-Varsity Fellowship, now the Universities and Colleges Christian
Fellowship, a student movement connecting Christian Unions in universities and colleges
throughout Great Britain, and a member movement of the International Fellowship of
Evangelical Students. Website: www.uccf.org.uk. That historic association is maintained,
and all senior IVP staff and committee members subscribe to the UCCF Basis of Faith.

To Robin and Alice Whaley,
partners in the gospel and dear friends

Contents

Preface and acknowledgments

Rarely have I been so gripped by the emotional power of an idea as this one: that Jesus is the Lover of my soul.

When I started delving into the spiritual meaning of the Song of Songs, I had little idea of the waves of love that would crash over my head. When I started preaching it, I was nervous – was it just me, or would others have a similar experience?

Some did struggle a bit with the poetry, but, for many, the love of Christ came alive in a striking new way. Jesus himself was making himself more real to us. I don't think any of us (including me) had experienced anything quite like it before, probably because the book is unique.

It is heady stuff – breathless love poetry, exotic settings, erotic imagery, word pictures that need some background explanation, the ups and downs of a relationship that is both human and divine. Sometimes it has felt as though I was eavesdropping on things almost too intimate and too sacred to be described. At other times I found myself wondering if Christ could really love me that much and say those sorts of things to me. Was it really OK to encourage people to see and feel that too? But, again and again, the spiritual meaning of the words hit home with fresh delights: yes, he did, and does.

There are superb commentaries on the Song of Songs; this is not another. There are fine explanations of what it says about human sexuality and marriage; I have not tried to add to them.

What I have done is to give extended treatment to the idea that Jesus loves me with the passion of a man for a woman, and that the Song of Songs illustrates this in extraordinary colours, scents and tastes, a music of words to set our souls on fire in response.

Many people have contributed directly and indirectly to the book. My heartfelt thanks to my beloved wife Debbie for her support in so many ways, and to everyone at Eden Baptist Church, Cambridge, for the time I have had for writing, prayer and study.

A number of friends who heard the sermons on the Song of Songs (the seedbed for this book) sent me comments on how the Song had affected their walk with Christ. Some of these are included, with changed names, in the text; many thanks to all of them. Yet again, I am grateful to Dr Amy Donovan, an expert on volcanoes and improving her pastor's writing, and also to Mark Meynell, Neil Thomson and Tim Chester who read the text with similar eagle eyes. An anonymous reader made many suggestions that led to improvements. I am full of gratitude to Eleanor Trotter, who has been a magnificent editor, and to Mollie Barker for her fine-grained copy-editing.

This book is dedicated to Robin and Alice Whaley, partners in the work of the gospel and friends in the love of Christ. In their walled fruit garden (like Song 4:12) in Kosovo, I met Christ more deeply as I studied the Song of Songs (summer 2018) and then wrote the first draft of this book (summer 2019). Their friendship and their garden identify them in a special way among the many friends Christ speaks of in Song 8:13:

> You who dwell in the gardens
>   with friends in attendance,
>   let me hear your voice!

This book is my response to Christ's words to me there. I must also mention Little Gidding, a special place for me, where this text was polished in high summer and repolished in early spring.

Above all, I am grateful to the Lord Jesus Christ, who revealed more of himself to me as the Lover of my soul, through the metaphor of spiritual marriage, in new and beautiful ways.

Julian Hardyman
Cambridge

1

Show me your face

Show me Thy face! – one transient gleam
Of loveliness divine,
And I shall never think or dream
Of other love save Thine;
All lesser light will darken quite,
All lower glories wane;
The beautiful of earth will scarce
Seem beautiful again.[1]

We used to sing this hymn in the church I joined when I started my working life. I had never heard it before. I love it and now include it in church services from time to time. When we sing it, we feel caught up in the writer's longing for a glimpse of the glory of Christ. As we read the words, we feel something stirring in our own souls.

Drawn by beauty

We feel ourselves being drawn into the words of Moses in Exodus 33:18: 'Show me your glory [that is, your beauty].' We remember Psalm 105:4:

Look to the LORD and his strength;
seek his face always.

Or Psalm 27:8:

My heart says of you, 'Seek his face!'
Your face, LORD, I will seek.

There is a beauty in the face of Christ which our renewed hearts long for. We want 'to gaze on the beauty of the LORD' (Psalm 27:4).

With that background, hear what the lover is saying to the beloved in Song 2:14:

> My dove in the clefts of the rock,
>   in the hiding-places on the mountainside,
> show me your face,
>   let me hear your voice;
> for your voice is sweet,
>   and your face is lovely.

The Song of Songs is doing the same thing as the rest of Scripture. It is a beautiful picture of human love, but it constantly points us beyond human intimacy to Jesus as the Lover of our souls.

My study of Jesus as the Lover of our souls draws most heavily on the Song of Songs. It is not an exposition of the Song, still less a commentary. It is written to help you to discover how Jesus is the Lover of your soul, and some of what that means for your relationship with him. It is like discovering a whole new world!

He's after me!

Seeking the face of Christ is entirely biblical, but the extraordinary thing is that this is about *Jesus'* longing to see *my* face. The man in the Song of Songs calls his beloved a 'dove' – he is a gazelle, but that is OK, as both are metaphors! The dove is not visible. She is hiding in a cleft in the rock of a stony outcrop on a mountain. But he is keen to see and hear her, so he calls to her to come out and show her face and coo back to him.

The young man uses this image to portray himself wanting to see his girlfriend's face and hear her speak. She is looking away and silent. Perhaps in modern terms she is absorbed in her smartphone! He wants eye contact. He longs for her attention. Why? Because her voice is so sweet to him. It is like his favourite music, his top song of all time. Hearing her speak thrills him – not just her voice in general, but all that it represents when she speaks to him: that she should want to talk to him!

And it is not just her voice. He longs to see her face. He finds her lovely. Her face pleases him aesthetically. When he sees it, there is a deep thrill in his gut, a kind of heady delight. Again, it is not simply her face in the abstract. It is her face turned towards him in love. How he longs to see her smile at him!

At the human level, this is a powerful portrayal of a lover longing for his beloved in deep appreciation. But we can and must take it a step further. This is Christ speaking to us, to you, to me. This is the voice of the heavenly Lover revealing his desire for his earthly beloved – you! Jesus himself says to your soul, 'Show me your face. Let me hear your voice. Your voice is sweet. Your face is lovely.'

Don't rush on too quickly. Pause there. Read these short simple sentences again. Pause between each part. Imagine Jesus himself saying these words to you today.

As you read and reread them in this way, pay attention to your reactions. So many people need to stop at that point and let this sink in. All sorts of objections start bubbling up in our minds. Surely this can't be right? Are we interpreting this correctly? How can this be true of me?

If you are in Christ, you can be sure that this does indeed apply to you, and that Christ himself says these words to you. As we have seen already, he desires us because he finds us desirable. These verses focus in a helpful and specific way on his desire for our attention and our speaking.

He wants you to turn your attention to him because he finds your face, your focused attention on him, 'lovely'. This reverses the normal reasons we have for focusing on Jesus. We tend to think of how we might benefit. We want him to help, please, soothe, maybe even delight us. And there is nothing wrong with any of that. We pray, 'O Lord, show me your face, let me hear your voice, for your voice is sweet and your face is lovely.' That is absolutely right too.

However, this is the other side of the relationship. He wants us! And, surely, we want to please him, to delight him, to satisfy him,

3

don't we? Of course we do. When we think of it, we want nothing more! The difficulty is believing that *he* wants *us*. But this verse tells us emphatically that he does. And we'd better believe it, however hard that can feel at first.

Dane Ortlund, in his book on the eighteenth-century American preacher Jonathan Edwards, puts it this way: 'Divine beauty is not only to be apprehended in God. It is to be reflected in us. It's why we exist.'[2]

You may well be wondering at this point what this looks like in practice. Now, I had never really noticed the verse above – 'My dove in the clefts of the rock . . . show me your face' – until I started studying the Song with a view to preaching sermons on the book. As I worked through the interpersonal drama of chapter 2, I realized that these were words that Christ was saying to me. Over the next few months they came to me repeatedly. The dialogue in the shaded box represents the way in which the Lord kept pressing his demands, his desires, on me.

Oh gosh, it's 7.30 already. I'm late. Too late for a quiet time. I suppose the Lord will understand.

Show me your face.

But I'm too busy.

Show me your face.

But you've got lots of other disciples – why can't you pick on one whose alarm clock went off on time?

Show me your face.

But I haven't had time to shave. Lots of people are not going to want to see my face at this rate!

Show me your face.

But I . . . I . . . My 'face' just isn't worth seeing.

Show me your face.

Lord, even I don't like my face very much, let alone what's behind it, and you have much higher standards than me.

Show me your face, for your face is lovely.

Oh no it's not. It's lopsided and blotchy and I've got revolting spots on my forehead.

Show me your face, for your face is lovely.

You aren't going to give up, are you, Lord?

Show me your face, for your face is lovely.

OK, I think you've got my attention now. But what can I say?

Let me hear your voice.

Well, I think that's happening, isn't it? I can't imagine you're enjoying it particularly, though . . .

Let me hear your voice, for your voice is sweet.

But I have a sore throat. And, seriously, all I'm doing is moaning.

Your voice is sweet.

OK, Lord, you win. This isn't about me, right? This is about you. You just want me! Well, I love you, and your face is beautiful to me, and your voice is lovelier than any other voice. Thank you.

Outworking

As part of our sermons on the Song of Songs at church, we had a 'Creative Responses to the Song' evening. I invited people to use their creativity to respond to what they had been hearing.

My own contribution was a self-portrait. I tried not to 'improve' anything. I wanted it to be the opposite of airbrushing. So I chose a photo in which I was not at my best. I had in mind the approach Rembrandt took to self-portraits, summed up in Oliver Cromwell's famous instruction to a painter:

Mr Lely, I desire you would use all your skill to paint my picture truly like me, and not flatter me at all; but remark all these roughnesses, pimples, warts and everything as you see me, otherwise I will never pay a farthing for it.[3]

I was happy that the portrait achieved what I wanted – a representation of how I often see myself. But, in spite of all that, I hear his voice saying, 'Let me see your face, let me hear your voice, for your voice is sweet, and your face is lovely.' It summed up the preceding eight months of growing closer to Christ. And as I showed him my face, I found him showing me his.

Chloe, a geography student from our church, shared this insight:

> My boyfriend gave me a small bookmark for my Bible with these verses written on it: 'Show me your face, let me hear your voice, for your voice is sweet, and your face is lovely.' He was giving me a physical reminder of the truth we were learning together: that Jesus invites me into a more intimate and more passionate and more truly satisfying relationship than any romantic human relationship. As Paul reminds us (for we so often forget), marriage mirrors Christ's relationship with the church (with me!), and it is that relationship with the Divine which contains truest intimacy and passion. This feels hard to fathom, and harder still to live out. However, it is also music to the ears of my generation, which is first and foremost a generation of the heart, longing for passionate and purposeful lives in which we love and are loved. As Ed Sheeran says: if you've known love in your life, then you've really lived.[4]

Christ asks us to turn our faces towards him because he loves the beauty he is creating there.

Dane Ortlund has another wonderful insight on this subject:

> The Christian life is a life of beauty. This is [Jonathan] Edwards's legacy. Love, joy, gentleness, prayer, obedience – all these . . . emphases are spokes extending from the hub of a soul alive to beauty. All are diverse manifestations of this single, fundamental reality. They are what healthy Christians exhale, having inhaled the loveliness of God.[5]

You have 'inhaled the loveliness of God'. Will you breathe out and let him savour the fragrance?

Voices

True prayer involves a journey down into the depths of our hearts to meet God in the totality of who we are. That is not an easy journey. We are easily distracted. So we use whatever it takes (getting alone, leaving the smartphone in the next room, turning off the music, sitting quietly, and perhaps even breathing deeply and slowly) to escape practical distractions.

But even then, there are voices that get in the way ('you're a deep disappointment to God') and layers of insecurity ('we are not sure that our true self will be acceptable to other people . . . And we are not sure that our inmost self is acceptable to us'[6]).

Many of us see our own ugly failings and try to take it out on ourselves. We are like the character in the novel *The Better Sister* by Alafair Burke, who had gained a public profile and found it impossible not to check her social networking feed: 'Catherine [her sister] had told me recently that my compulsive need to read the horrid things that anonymous strangers wrote about me online evidenced a subconscious desire to punish myself.'[7]

This character is looking for negative and destructive voices. While we all need to be open to correction and to constructive feedback, too many of us Christians are also listening to the wrong voices.

The voices are hard to ignore because we have been listening to them for so long. The layers are difficult to penetrate; we have set them up as defences, after all. This reminds me of the song 'Sam's Town' by The Killers, where someone says he is sick of being judged all the time, living in fear of what people might find out about him.[8]

That is where a Scripture text like this will help us if we understand it as part of the gospel. We look outside ourselves at the free gift of Christ's righteousness. Then we look within. Not for one moment does it undercut our understanding of our own sinfulness and our need for self-examination and repentance. But it enables us to respond as people clothed, covered and cleansed by the righteousness of Christ, and as people whose ugliness really is being changed into something beautiful by Christ, and for Christ's own delight. For even the sight of a tear-stained face, stammering out our own humble acknowledgment of our sin, our hatred of it and our plea for his forgiveness rather than trying to manufacture our own, is beautiful and lovely to him.

Questions

- What are your major obstacles to hearing and receiving Jesus saying the words of Song 2:14 to you?
- How can you lay these obstacles to one side?

Think about how these words can work in your life when you don't feel great about yourself, and when you come to church but are quite disengaged from the Lord.

Prayer

Lord, these words are almost too much for me. I do find it hard to believe them consistently. How can they be true? How can you want my attention? How can you long for me to speak to you? But I know that your Word is true. I want to hear this and receive it. Help me.

Thank you. Thank you that, in Christ, this is true. This is how you hear me and see me. As I take this seriously, I feel something hard and cold melting inside. I feel tense fears lurking within me being relaxed and soothed. At the same time, I feel myself being taken outside myself, to focus less on myself, as though I am being removed from the centre of things and replaced by you and your desires. I turn to you in willing surrender and love: I want you to have as much of me as I can give. Amen.

2

A supremely satisfying intimacy

Have you ever sung the popular Kari Jobe song 'Jesus, Lover of My Soul'[1] in church and stopped to think about what that phrase actually means?

Or you may have sung an older hymn that starts:

Jesus, Lover of my soul,
let me to thy bosom fly . . .[2]

If the first line of this hymn seems odd, then the second seems odder still. For a start, 'bosom' is not a word we use much, and when we do, it's a word for a *woman's* chest, not a man's, and also, the picture of flying to Jesus' bosom isn't self-evidently a spiritually helpful one.

For most of us, let's be honest, it feels strange to address Jesus as a romantic partner – a lover, fiancé, bridegroom, even a husband.

I have written this book because Jesus as Lover of our souls is one of the great pictures God has given us for his love, because many Christians hardly understand it, and because it has great power to take us deeper in our relationship with him. We find the picture throughout the Bible, and most especially in the Song of Songs, which is at the heart of my book.

What does love look like?

'God *is* love' is a wonderful statement. And 'God loves *you*' is a wonderful thing to realize. But abstract words only get us so far. Both statements need content (what does this kind of love do and mean?) and comparison (what kind of love is this? What does it look like?). God knows well that we need metaphors and similes and pictures and comparisons from the world we see and the lives we live. These show us in concrete ways that he is love and what it is like to be loved by him.

In two of his shorter parables in the Gospels, Jesus uses the metaphor of treasure and pearls to show how desirable he is:

> The kingdom of heaven is like treasure hidden in a field. When a man found it, he hid it again, and then in his joy went and sold all he had and bought that field.
>
> Again, the kingdom of heaven is like a merchant looking for fine pearls. When he found one of great value, he went away and sold everything he had and bought it.
> (Matthew 13:44–46)

The man and the merchant go insane when they find the treasure and the pearl. It is the ultimate Treasure, and the Pearl of pearls. Their reaction is like the insanity of romantic passion. It reminds me of Bruce Springsteen's best-known song, 'Born to Run', where he sings to an imaginary girlfriend about loving her with all the madness in his soul.[3]

That is the craziness of romantic love.[4] That is the passion of a woman who breathes, 'Let him kiss me with the kisses of his mouth, for your love is better than wine.'[5] Christ is so infinitely sweet and beautiful and satisfying as to evoke a deep longing and a wild, mad desire. He wants us to love him with all the madness our souls are capable of. Human desire, human romance, crazy human love . . . all point us to something greater: Christ's love for us, and the love he wants to give us for himself.

Pictures of God

The Bible is full of different pictures for God and how he relates to us: a rock, an angry bear, a fierce lion, a well-fortified tower, a powerful wind, a warming and life-giving sun, fresh spring water, a staple food, a shadow in hot weather, healing balm for a wound, the head of a household, a gardener, the keeper of a vineyard, the captain of an army, a breastfeeding mother, an older brother, a devoted father.

Every aspect of creation points in one way or another to some truth about God as he relates to us. Solid and even dense though a mountain may be, it is like a shadow of the sheer vastness of God. The whole created order and the whole human world – real though they are, of course – were created to portray spiritual realities greater than themselves.

Two supreme images

All the images matter. But God has given us two family metaphors that stand at the head of all the others in their power to evoke our longing – and meet it in the gospel.

The first is God as Father (which includes Jesus as our older Brother, Hebrews 2:11–12). This is one of the most important pictures in Scripture. It has been well explored in wonderful books on the Lord's Prayer,[6] as well as in many other places.

The other is the Lover/Bridegroom/Husband: Christ as our *Lover* (with us as his beloved/bride/wife). Just as the Father picture is rich with implications for us, so the Lover picture is too. Because it is different, it takes us to places that even the Father picture cannot reach. It touches on a place deep within us that longs for someone to love *us* 'with all the madness in his or her soul'. God, in his wise but to us often strange planning of our lives, may or may not give us a man or a woman to desire and love like that. But he has planned our lives so that we discover that his Son loves us like that, and for us to enjoy loving him in return.

An undiscovered country

The biblical picture of Christ as the Lover of our souls is like undiscovered territory for most of us. Almost every Christian has heard many sermons on God as Father, and found huge help in them and in similar Bible studies. But I have found very few Christians who have thought much, if anything at all, about Jesus as the Lover of their soul. Fewer still have explored the rich implications in their actual felt, day-by-day, moment-by-moment relationship with Christ. And there are plenty of Christians who have sung songs about Jesus as the Lover and felt a bit uncomfortable. (We will come to that later.)

So, I am inviting you into undiscovered territory, a place rich with spiritual meaning and potential. This book is intended to draw you into a deeper understanding and experience of the love of Christ within this special, unique biblical metaphor, to know a greater, more lasting, more satisfying intimacy – with Jesus Christ himself, as seen especially in the Song of Songs.

When we looked at the Song of Songs in my church, one person described it as 'keeping us from grey unbelief, in a higher, purer and enrapturing love'. (Yes, sometimes even belief can become a bit grey!) Another commented:

> I think the majority of input most students and young adults receive on their personal relationship with Christ is actually pretty thin gruel – essentially, 'Make sure you have a daily time of Bible reading and prayer!', and then perhaps in more conservative circles, lots of assertions about how wonderful it is to read the Bible every day, and in more charismatic ones, a big emphasis on seeking the presence of God in worship and prayer, which is then not very easy to take home into their one-to-one time with the Lord. Essentially, I think there's a huge need and appetite for genuinely biblical guidance on going deeper in the dynamics of relationship with Christ, which are recognizably what we mean when we say 'relational'.

We have found that this is important and enriching for single as well as married people:

> As a single person, it would be easy to think that the Song of Songs wouldn't have much to say to me. [But it] presented to me both a challenge and an invitation to press on deeper into the love that Christ has for his beloved.

Frances, a student, shares the effect that understanding the Song of Songs can have:

> When I became a Christian, I knew I had a restored relationship with God but I didn't really understand what people meant when they talked about their relationship with Jesus. I knew he had died on the cross for me, but it confused me. I had no idea that there were such riches to be found in my relationship with him. Delving into spiritual intimacy with him is so needed! Through [understanding the spiritual marriage metaphor] this year, I have uncovered new joys that I had not known or expected.

My heartfelt prayer for you as reader is that these pages will give you new joys you have not known or expected, through a fuller knowledge of the high-octane, full-spectrum, richly spiced love of Christ as your divine Lover, and you as his beloved.

Questions

- What reaction do you have to the idea of seeing Christ as Lover/Bridegroom/Husband?
- Are you able to view your relationship with him as a spiritual 'romance' and 'marriage'?

Prayer

Lord, thank you for all the pictures of yourself and your love in the Bible. Thank you that every single one matters. Help me to understand the picture of spiritual romance and marriage – even though it is hard sometimes. Amen.

3

Desire: you're the one that I want!

When the *Voyager* spacecraft was being prepared for its launch in 1977, a recording was included to represent planet earth. The final track was a movement, the Cavatina, from a string piece by Beethoven.[1]

It is a lovely piece of music, but it was the *word* that Beethoven wrote on the manuscript that mattered most: the German term *Sehnsucht*, which means 'deep longing'. It was an excruciating time in Beethoven's life. His deafness, a terrible affliction for a musician, was affecting him deeply. He had had a long-standing passion for a woman much younger than him, but it was unrequited. While writing this piece, he wrote in a letter, 'O God, without a wife, and what an existence.' And as he composed, he poured his desire into the music.

The centre of your soul

Longing and desire are at the centre of our existence, the very centre of our souls. We are incomplete; we long for more. And more than anything, we long for personal intimacy – closeness with other people. Perhaps highest of all, we long for the romantic, sexual intimacy of marriage, but our longing is not confined to that.

Longing is where the Song of Songs, the greatest song ever written,[2] starts, with the abrupt explosion of desire:

Let him kiss me with the kisses of his mouth –
   for your love is more delightful than wine.
(Song 1:2)

It is unashamed, restless, expectant – like a young chick in a nest opening its beak pointedly and noisily for its mother to feed it. We sense this young woman's longing. She wants her man. She wants him to kiss her. His lovemaking is better than the very best wine.

Simply the best

One December I was feeling a bit gloomy because my wife was quite unwell. A friend turned up unexpectedly and thrust two bottles at me. 'Something to cheer you up,' he said, and grinned sympathetically. The gift was identical bottles of vintage port, bottled in 1970. His parents had bought him a number of cases (each containing twelve bottles). They had 'laid them down' – to be drunk when they had matured properly and were at their best.

Thirty-two years on, they were at their best. I discovered online that this was a very special vintage. I wondered for a moment about selling them online, but decided that wasn't really in the spirit of the gift. But keeping them to myself didn't quite seem in the spirit of the gift either. So, after our last leaders' meeting of the year, we each enjoyed a small glass of this nectar.

I had a sip and thought: I can honestly say that this is the best port I have ever drunk. Then I had another sip and thought: this is the best drink of any kind I have ever drunk. Then another sip and, possibly getting a bit carried away, I said, 'This is not just better than any other drink I have ever drunk; it is better than all the other drinks I have ever drunk put together.'

I could still taste it on my tongue by memory a year later. I can even summon up the taste memory now, and it sits pleasingly on some sensitive part of the virtual tongue of the imagination.

Your turn now! Think of your equivalent. The best day out. The best swim. The best restaurant meal. The best concert. The best ice cream. The best evening in the pub. The best sunset. I am not trying to take the joy of those experiences away from you, but this young woman in the Song of Songs stands for us all when she says, 'Your love is better than wine.' We are people; the best things of this world do not match the love of another human being.

The Bible teaches us that this longing and desire is right and good – something we see from Adam's gasp of delight at his first sight of Eve onwards. And it teaches that the most intimate and delightful love is found in the exclusive, sexual and lifelong love of a man and a woman in marriage (Genesis 2:18–25). It starts with a longing that drives and impels people forward in a kind of madness. We long to experience what poets and rock lyricists write about – like Meatloaf, whose knees felt weak in the embrace of his girlfriend while his soul was flying high above him.[3]

This feeling represents a longing that starts to stir in adolescence, and that pretty well all human beings have to work out at each stage of their lives. It is the sort of longing God has made us to experience. It shouts and whispers to us about 'the completion of ourselves from beyond ourselves'.[4]

The meaning of desire

God has his own purposes in putting this longing there, deep within us. It *may* be to draw us into a human relationship which would otherwise threaten our independence too much. Whether it has that effect or not in our lives, for all of us it can point to something beyond human love that is even richer and fuller.

But, let's face it, the Christian church has not always been comfortable with human physical and emotional desires. It has often spoken about them as though they were necessary evils to get men and women to make vows of commitment and to produce children – as though such desires were like some young plant that could easily produce sweet-tasting but poisonous fruit, and so were best stamped on, rather than carefully trained up the right trellis to be enabled to flower at the right time and in the right place.

Song 1:2, with its sudden burst of longing, shows us that God is positive about desire; indeed, it is God-given in the first place! One pastor says rather provocatively:

When the woman in the song [of songs] dreams of her boyfriend, she does not imagine them sharing an inductive Bible study and praying together, but thinks about his kisses and caresses. It is precisely this desire that her community celebrates.[5]

At this point my greatest fear is that some readers will find this topic too sensitive to want to go any further. I do understand your hesitation. But may I invite you to continue on the basis that *the book you are reading is not about human relationships*, but our relationship with Christ? There really is more here of Christ for you (as there is too for people in romantic relationships or marriages).

Ultimate longings

Even this love, which is better than the best of the rest of created things, is not the full and ultimate meaning of this text. It points to a desire that underlies all other desires, one that will not ever, cannot ever, be fully satisfied in this world because it was not designed to be satisfied in this world. It was designed to awaken a longing deep within us that can only be satisfied by Christ.

What a teacher wrote to me about young people is also true of all of us:

It's no secret that our young people are somewhat lost when it comes to understanding relationships and intimacy. Conflicting messages come at them from all angles of secular society, and many struggle deeply with self-esteem and direction. The message of ultimate fulfilment through spiritual intimacy with Christ is much needed.

These words, 'Let him kiss me with the kisses of his mouth', legitimize our human longing for passionate intimacy with another human person. But the Bible as a whole insists that that is not the goal of our deepest longings, and even the best of husbands or wives will never meet that longing. Only Christ, in personal intimacy, will do so. We have to look for completion from beyond ourselves, and even beyond the joys of marriage. It is this realization that David reached when he was feeling particularly sorry for himself:

Whom have I in heaven but you?
And earth has nothing I desire besides you.
(Psalm 73:25)

Infinite beauty

David has come by quite a journey to this point. The route has been over broken glass with no sandals on. God is simply matchless. God is ultimate beauty. Satisfaction in God is the highest satisfaction.

If you have Christ's love and don't have the relationship(s) of intimacy, married or otherwise, in this life, you still have infinitely more than someone who is happily married with children and lots of friends. Infinitely more. If you are married, and/or have children and lots of friends, Christ is infinitely more precious and beautiful than any of them, good though those relationships are. Desire is God-given and leads us to Christ.

Questions

- What do you think of the idea that all desire only finds its true satisfaction in Christ?
- What happens when you put that idea alongside your relational, romantic, sexual and other desires?

Prayer

Lord, this talk of desire has touched me in some places that are sensitive. A lot of the time, I try not to go there because it feels as though it uncages a tiger or removes a piece of armour that keeps me nicely protected. But I want to offer you the whole of who I am, including my capacity for desire. As I do that, I want to hear what you say about romantic desire being good but not ultimate. And I thank you that you are the Ultimately Desirable One. Will you show me what that means for both of us as I read this book? Amen.

4

Jesus is the
Lover of my soul . . .

In recent years a number of Christian worship songs have been written in which people sing to Jesus as though he was a human lover.[1] Occasionally the lyrics sound like the latest single from Taylor Swift. The writers take the kinds of things that someone might sing in a romantic song – the lover is 'so beautiful, so adorable' – and invite Christians to sing them.

Inevitably the quality varies, and in response a lot of people object: 'I really don't get on with the "Jesus is my boyfriend" kind of song.' It is true that some of the songs are rather syrupy and sentimental. And you have to admit that it is strange thinking about someone you are not in a romantic relationship with and then singing about that person in church! But, having agreed, I find myself wanting to add, 'Yes, I see what you mean, but . . .'

This book is about the 'but' in that sentence. The tradition of worship songs addressing Jesus as Lover or Husband is actually centuries old. But for most of us, it feels *strange* to think of Jesus as a romantic partner – a suitor, a lover, a husband. How much more natural to think of God as Father (though some can struggle with that too, for understandable reasons), or to see Jesus as our Master, Shepherd – or even our older Brother.

But God himself appears to have thought that using the picture of a lover with his beloved, and a husband with his wife, was one that we could not only cope with, but learn important things from. After all, as we will see, he uses it a great deal!

Come with me on a whistle-stop tour from Genesis right through to Revelation.

In the beginning

From Genesis 1 – 2 onwards, marriage is central in human society. It is between a man and a woman; it is lifelong, exclusive and sexual – and marriage is the only right setting for sexual relationships. A wedding is 'the ceremony that celebrates the unique joining of intimacy and faithfulness that is marriage'.[2] This includes the special joys of sexual love, but also the unbreakable commitment of one to another. It therefore provides a particularly powerful metaphor to understand God's relationship with his people. Yet, as Paul says in Ephesians 5, marriage was always about more than human love in the Bible, always pointing to God's love and our response.

Spiritual marriage gone sour

However, often in the Old Testament the metaphor of spiritual marriage is used sadly and reproachfully to demonstrate how serious Israel's sin is, by comparing idolatry to adultery. We find this early in the records of the nation's history. In the incident of the golden calf, the Lord speaks of his jealousy in response – the kind of jealousy a husband rightly has for his wife.[3]

In the era of the prophets, the marriage metaphor really comes into its own. Isaiah, Jeremiah, Ezekiel, and above all Hosea, accuse Israel of indulging in *adulterous* behaviour by worshipping other gods:

'Return, faithless people,' declares the LORD, 'for I am your husband.'
(Jeremiah 3:14)

'But like a woman unfaithful to her husband, so you, Israel, have been unfaithful to me,' declares the LORD.
(Jeremiah 3:20)

Note both the metaphor: 'I am your husband', and the simile: 'like a woman unfaithful to her husband'. In the Old Testament this imagery is most often used negatively, to reproach Israel. But it is also used positively, as in:

> For your Maker is your husband . . .
> the Holy One of Israel is your Redeemer . . .
> (Isaiah 54:5)

Also notice the connection between the marriage image and redemption – rescue from sin, a new beginning with a new master. Salvation is pictured as marriage. We see this again in Isaiah 62, where God's new work of redemption (fulfilled in Christ) is portrayed as a woman becoming a bride, with God as the Bridegroom:

> As a young man marries a young woman,
>   so will your Builder marry you;
> as a bridegroom rejoices over his bride,
>   so will your God rejoice over you.
> (Isaiah 62:5)

Into the New Testament

This pattern of imagery provides Jesus with a palette to paint himself with (just as he does with other Old Testament images, like shepherd, bread, water and wine). So, when Jesus calls himself a 'bridegroom' (Matthew 9:15; John 3:29), or describes the kingdom of heaven as like a king preparing a wedding banquet for his son (Matthew 22:1–2) or ten virgins going out to meet the bridegroom (Matthew 25:1), everyone knows where the picture is coming from.

Paul picks up the same imagery in Ephesians 5, and explores its depths:

> The husband is the head of the wife as Christ is the head of the church, his body, of which he is the Saviour. Now as the church submits to Christ, so also wives should submit to their husbands in everything.

Husbands, love your wives, just as Christ loved the church and gave himself up for her to make her holy, cleansing her by the washing with water through the word, and to present her to himself as a radiant church, without stain or wrinkle or any other blemish, but holy and blameless.
(Ephesians 5:23–27)

For Paul, Genesis is about more than male–female relationships; it is about Jesus and his people. He is our Husband; we are his wife – a 'profound mystery' (Ephesians 5:32) but a vital reality. Geoffrey Bromiley puts it this way: 'As God made man in His own image, so He made earthly marriage in the image of His own eternal marriage with His people.'[4]

Sometimes we are seen as already married to Jesus, but often we are engaged, and getting ready for the great event of our lives, our wedding day. That seems to be the line of thought in 2 Corinthians 11:2: 'I am jealous for you with a godly jealousy. I promised you to one husband, to Christ, so that I might present you as a pure virgin to him.' Then sometimes we see the future marriage of Revelation 19:

Let us rejoice and be glad
 and give him glory!
For the wedding of the Lamb has come,
 and his bride has made herself ready . . .

Blessed are those who are invited to the wedding supper of the Lamb!
(Revelation 19:7–9)

These references show that the marriage relationship is a highly significant picture of Christ's relationship with his people. In fact Ray Ortlund states: 'Marriage is the wraparound concept for the entire Bible . . . the Bible is telling a story of married romance.'[5] That means that we ought to make attempts to understand its weight and importance! If God uses it so much, then surely he has something unique to show us through this metaphor.

Beloved, bride, wife – all of us, and me individually

As we read these texts carefully, we can see that the metaphor portrays the Lord (Old Testament) or Jesus (New Testament) as the Lover/Bridegroom/Husband, and the people of God (Old Testament) or church (New Testament) as the beloved/bride/wife. That is a correct and undoubtedly an important way of applying this set of pictures – to the church universal through all time, to the church universal on earth at any phase of history, to the church in any country or region, to the church in any city or locality – and to individual local churches too.

However, there are biblical data to suggest that applying the metaphor to *individual* believers is also right – and by that, I mean seeing Jesus as the Lover of *your* soul. A prime example is in James 4:4: 'You adulterous people, don't you know that friendship with the world means enmity against God?' In the New International Version there is a helpful footnote to the phrase 'adulterous people' which reads: 'An allusion to covenant unfaithfulness; see Hosea 3:1'. The same word is used there, where the Lord is telling Hosea to reach out to his unfaithful wife, Gomer. The New American Standard Bible more simply translates James's words as 'You adulteresses . . .'. Each of them (men and women) is being taken to task for his or her sin, which makes each person *individually* unfaithful to Christ, the divine Lover and Husband.

Set free

Then, in Romans 7, Paul uses the marriage analogy again for our pre-conversion relationship with the law of Moses and our post-conversion relationship with Jesus:

> By law a married woman is bound to her husband as long as he is alive, but if her husband dies, she is released from the law that binds her to him. So then, if she has sexual relations with another man while her husband is still alive, she is called an

adulteress. But if her husband dies, she is released from that law and is not an adulteress if she marries another man.

So, my brothers and sisters, you also died to the law through the body of Christ, that you might belong to another, to him who was raised from the dead . . .

(Romans 7:2–4)

Our relationship with the law is so binding that it is as though we are married to it. Such a tight relationship can only be ended by death – so we are stuck! But, in Christ, we 'die to the law', and so we are set free from that otherwise indissoluble tie. Our new freedom through this death releases us to 'belong to another' – and Paul means Christ. Paul's analogy only makes sense if it is applied to us individually.

United with Christ

Paul again uses marriage language for our individual relationship with Christ in 1 Corinthians 6:15–16, though it is subtle.[6] In dealing with the problem of Christians in Corinth having sexual intercourse with prostitutes, Paul says that there is no such thing as casual sex: all sex has some relationship to sex within marriage, which is simultaneously the expression and the sealing of the exclusive closeness of marriage summed up in Genesis 2:24 as 'one flesh'. He clinches his argument in a remarkable way: 'Whoever is united with the Lord is one with him in spirit' (1 Corinthians 6:17).

Ray Ortlund puts it this way: 'The Christian has been brought into spiritual union with the Lord, analogous to sexual union. Paul's language requires the analogy to be drawn.'[7]

Sex with a prostitute makes the believer 'one with [the prostitute's] body', which is wrong and horrendous. In married sex, by contrast, a man and a woman become 'one flesh', which is good and right. But even 'one flesh' falls short of being one 'in spirit' with the Lord Jesus.

Here is Ortlund again: 'The believer is even more intimate with the Lord than with his or her spouse, for this is a union of spirit, and spirit always leads one more deeply into reality than does flesh.'[8]

A helpful picture

Another reason for seeing the image as applying to individuals, as well as whole churches, is suggested by a seventeenth-century vicar called Richard Sibbes in his sermons on the Song of Songs. He argues from the nature of what he calls 'homogeneal bodies'(!), where there is a much closer relationship between one part and the whole than there would be, say, between your toenail and your whole body. Much of what is true of the ocean is true of a drop of water, and what is true of a large fire is true of a single flame. What is true of the whole is true of the similar, micro parts of the whole. 'Therefore,' he says, 'as the whole church is the spouse of Christ, so is every particular Christian; and as the whole church desires still nearer communion with Christ, so does every particular member.'[9]

Charles Spurgeon, the famous Victorian Baptist preacher, builds on this:

> Each saint may say, 'This belongs to me.' That which belongs to the redeemed family belongs to each member of that family. That which is true of light is true of each beam, that which is true of water is true of each drop, and that which is true of the church as a whole is true of each member of that mystical body. Jesus loves each one of His people with that same love with which He loves the whole of His people.[10]

So, we may take the image of Jesus as our Lover *individually* as well as corporately. This provokes a number of questions. If the individual reading is intended, what is the practical value? Does the Bible help us to understand *how* Jesus is the Lover of our souls, or do we just have to work it out from the way romantic relationships and marriages work generally? My answer is that this is why the Song of Songs is in the Bible.

Listen to Giselle, a recent university graduate, commenting on this:

> The notion of spiritual intimacy with Jesus, for the Christian, is not only deeply biblically founded but also unendingly

beautiful. The importance of a relationship with Jesus is an area that has been explored by many evangelical writers, but a deeper exploration of the richness and fulfilling beauty of this relationship, expounded through biblical metaphor, would be very edifying. Recently, I had the privilege of [hearing more about this picture] for several weeks, and during that time my personal understanding of the intimacy of God's relationship with me grew immensely.

Questions

- How do you feel about the idea of spiritual marriage, with Jesus being your divine Lover?
- If you find it difficult in some way, why not review the argument for this being a picture which God himself gives us – and then ask God to help you receive this picture and experience what he wants to give you through it?

Prayer

Lord Jesus, I deeply appreciate your love for me, and it is so helpful that you give me lots of pictures from human and physical life so that I can understand it better. But this picture is less easy to live in than most of the others. I do want to know your love better. Please help me to understand this picture, and to receive this picture, and by the work of your Spirit to know more of your love through it. Amen.

5

Us: how the Song of Songs is about Jesus and me

I was sitting in the garden of one of the best biblical studies libraries in the world, eating lunch with an old friend.[1] We were catching up after a long absence but with limited time (he had to get back to work). We talked mostly, would you believe it, about the Song of Songs.

'I've memorized quite a bit,'[2] he said, rather shyly, not wanting to boast. 'It's my favourite book of the Bible.'

'Really?' I replied. 'I thought it was Isaiah' (a book he had spent three years studying intensively).

'No, not Isaiah. The Song.'

He then became rather inarticulate, not from embarrassment or a lack of clarity, but because this was such precious, holy ground for him. It was his favourite biblical book because there he found more about Christ's love than anywhere else. I knew exactly what he meant. I believe that the Song of Songs is the key text for understanding and experiencing Jesus as the Lover of your soul.

On the face of it, the Song of Songs is a collection of love poems. My approach is to read the Song of Songs as this, *and also, and more importantly*, as being about our relationship with Christ.

Many people have argued against this approach. They say that the Song doesn't mention God (except for one rather disputed possibility in 8:6[3]). They say that the 'spiritual' way of reading it devalues the human relationship and human bodies, and ends up with very strange interpretations.

Almost everyone points to the way an early church father, Gregory of Nyssa (c. 335 – c. 395), interprets Song 1:13:

My beloved is to me a sachet of myrrh
  resting between my breasts.

Gregory sees Jesus as the sachet of myrrh, with one breast representing the Old Testament and the other representing the New! The problem is that this method of reading it, given the way the text is allegorized, is uncontrolled. When you read many spiritual interpretations, both older and newer, there is a lot of rather fanciful explanation of the minute details of the text, even in some of the best.

However, just as the fact that a few students drop out of university shouldn't put someone off applying, so the fact of poor spiritualization doesn't mean that we shouldn't attempt to do careful, restrained and cautious work to try to find and hear the voice of Christ in the Song of Songs.

Six biblical reasons for this spiritual reading

1 Christ is in all the Old Testament

Jesus himself explained after his resurrection that the entire Old Testament pointed to him in his incarnation, atonement and resurrection: '[Jesus] said to them, "This is what I told you while I was still with you: everything must be fulfilled that is written about me in the Law of Moses, the Prophets and the Psalms"' (Luke 24:44). While the Song of Songs is not explicitly mentioned in the phrase 'the Law, the Prophets and the Psalms', Jesus is best understood as referring here to the entire Old Testament. The metaphor of 'spiritual marriage' is pervasive in both the Old and New Testament for our relationship with God.

This was the point of the previous chapter. The Song is set in a context where we expect romance and marriage to show us about Christ. It is not alien to the pattern of romance and marital imagery we find in the Bible for salvation; arguably, it completes it.

2 The title of the book

Our first piece of evidence in the Song of Songs itself suggesting that it is about more than purely human love is in the title. The book calls itself the 'Song of Songs'. (It is a mistake to call it the 'Song of Solomon'.) This is a bigger claim than we tend to realize at first reading. The form of words 'X of X' denotes a superlative, used in the Old Testament for the highest version of whatever is being described; for example: 'God of gods and Lord of lords' (Deuteronomy 10:17), 'vanity of vanities' (Ecclesiastes 1:2 NRSV), 'king of kings' (Ezra 7:12).

So, for this Song to call itself 'Song of Songs' is a very big claim. The text itself is claiming to be the greatest song ever written, including all the songs in the Bible. But if it is merely about human love and intimacy, that means it is claiming that those are greater than the divine love praised in Psalm 111 and elsewhere. That would be idolatrous and blasphemous. And that is what human beings have so often done, not least in today's society: set romantic and sexual passion as their highest goal. But the Bible does not allow that; God is our highest goal. So, the very title of the Song of Songs indicates that it must be about more than human love.

3 The land, the landscape and its images

The Song locates itself in an idealized natural and cultivated land-scape of beauty and fruitfulness, using images from this landscape to describe the beauty of bride and groom, and their love. The setting is the Promised Land of Israel, with real landmarks like the tower of David. It is the beautiful land, the place of God's blessing for his people. At times the Song seems to celebrate the land as much as, if not more than, the physical beauty of the man and the woman. As the Song portrays the woman as a physical landscape (for example, 4:1–7; 6:4–9; 7:1–9), it pushes us towards seeing her as representing the people of God. We find a deeper meaning than simply a human love; the land was beloved to God and married to God:

> You will be called Hephzibah ['my delight is in her'],
>   and your land Beulah ['married'];

for the LORD will take delight in you,
    and your land will be married.
(Isaiah 62:4)

4 The royal wedding theme

Another feature of the Song is the idea of the king who marries his bride. The lover (whether Solomon or not) is portrayed as kingly (for example, 1:12; 3:7–10; 5:10–16). This points us towards Psalm 45, Solomon's wedding psalm and the closest kind of literature to the Song anywhere else in the Bible, a song of praise to an idealized king (too perfect to be any merely human king) on his wedding day. Tellingly, in the New Testament, Psalm 45 is applied to Jesus (Hebrews 1:8–9). The natural move is to follow suit and do the same with the Song.

5 Balancing the 'unfaithful wife' theme

As we have seen, in the Old Testament Israel is often portrayed as God's unfaithful wife who is disloyal to him. Strikingly, five of the six Bible books that follow the Song use the theme of the unfaithful wife prominently. There are numerous verbal echoes of these books in the Song of Songs; whichever might have been written first, it feels as though these echoes are tying the different texts together. One example is the term the woman uses for herself in Song 2:1: a 'rose of Sharon' (probably a type of crocus). The only other place in the Bible where we find that flower mentioned is Isaiah 35:1–2:

The wilderness will rejoice and blossom.
Like the *crocus*, it will burst into bloom . . .[4]

It makes perfect sense for the theme of the unfaithful wife to be balanced by a picture of the same relationship, but in this case working well.

6 The hyperbolic idealization of love in the Song

As we will see, love is viewed in idealized terms in the Song, beyond the aspirations and expectations of any human relationship.

Particularly in Song chapter 8, claims are made for it that human love simply cannot fulfil. It must therefore be about more than human love.

These arguments build a cumulative, persuasive case.

A long tradition

Now let me show you that the 'divine love' interpretation is no novelty. In the history of how the Song has been applied, it has been what is known as 'the majority position'. Jewish interpreters saw the text as a picture of God and his people. Among them some took it 'mystically', as being about *individual* relationships with God. One renowned rabbi, Akiba, called the Song of Songs the 'Holy of Holies'.

Virtually all Christian interpreters until the Reformation and later were nervous about the human interpretation (they were nervous about sex generally), and so applied it only to Christ and the church – and by extension, to Christ and the individual believer. That led to a great deal of writing and preaching on the Song of Songs. For example, between the fourth and eleventh centuries we have six surviving commentaries written in Latin on Galatians, four on Romans, and thirty-two on the Song. The book continued to be much studied in the medieval church. One of the classic devotional works is Bernard of Clairvaux's eighty-eight sermons on the Song of Songs.[5]

After the Reformation the Song started to be read as a human love song/story, but preachers continued to preach it 'spiritually'.[6] In nineteenth-century London Charles Spurgeon preached over sixty sermons on the Song. But this preaching became less common in the twentieth century. It seems as though the Song became comparatively neglected. However, since the sexual revolution of the 1960s there has been something of a revival of interest, with many evangelical preachers and writers focused only on the human interpretation. The Song has been seen as a kind of marriage guide, even a sex manual ('Solomon on Sex'), with sermon series using titles like 'The Joy of Sex – Bible-style'.[7]

What the Song does

The Song of Songs makes us aware of our drive for personal intimacy, and shows the right place for that desire for intimacy – in the close, committed, joyful, exclusive and sexual relationship of marriage. It teaches us about our desires and our search for that close connection. That means that it can be a useful, but also a hard, book for single people.

The Song tells us that whether single or married, our experience of human relationships will never match that of the lovers in the Song, nor be enough to fully satisfy us. It makes us long for a more than merely human intimacy, and gives a dramatic framework for us to experience that intimacy with Christ. Its poetry stimulates our imaginations to see how Christ loves us.

A song of wisdom

The Song has links to the Old Testament book of Proverbs, especially through its mention of Solomon and its much-repeated vocabulary and themes. It is particularly close to Proverbs 5 – 9, a section that is addressed to young men and is largely about sex and relationships, and being wise about both. The Song of Songs is the equivalent for young women: about finding a man, waiting for the right time, looking for someone like the Solomonic ideal, but better than the actual Solomon – neither a fool (easily seduced) nor the kind of king who sees relationships as a tool of diplomacy or lust.[8] But the Song also speaks to young men, and for both men and women of all ages it is more than wisdom about relationships. As Iain Duguid explains:

> The Song show[s] us an idealized picture of married love, in the context of a fallen and broken world. As it does so, it intends to convict each of us of how far short of this perfection we fall, both as humans and as lovers, and thus to drive us repeatedly into the arms of our true heavenly husband, Jesus Christ . . . The Song speaks to us as whole people, in need of wisdom in our relationships with other human beings and in

our relationship with God ... Our broken human relationships tell us something about our broken relationship with God (1 John 4:20), but the remedy for our failed loves is to be found always and only in God's unfailing love.[9]

Matthew Henry (1662–1714), in his famous *Commentary on the Whole Bible*, put it this way:

> There are depths that an elephant may swim in here. It requires some pains to find out what may probably be the meaning of the Holy Spirit in the several parts of this book. But when the meaning is found out, it will be of admirable use to excite pious and devout affections in us, and the same to the soul with a pleasing power. When we apply ourselves to the study of this book, we must not only put off our shoes from off our feet and even forget that we have bodies[!], because the place we stand is holy ground, but we must come up hither, must spread our wings, take a noble flight and soar upwards till by faith and holy love we enter into the holiest, for this is no other than the house of God and this is the gate of heaven.[10]

But, let's be honest, many of us wonder how God could love us and want us near him. We will look at that in the next chapter.

Questions

- Do you find the argument that the Song should be read as portraying divine–human love as well as human marriage persuasive?
- What do you think of the suggestion that, within this metaphor, we can apply Christ's love not only to the church in general but also to ourselves individually?

Prayer

Lord, help me to hear your voice speaking to me as the Lover of my soul. Amen.

6

Insecurity: will you still love me tomorrow?

The photographer John Rankin Waddell, better known as Rankin, has described an interesting experiment which he ran:

> For my latest series, Selfie Harm, I photographed teenagers and handed them the image to then edit and filter until they felt it was 'social-media ready'. People are mimicking their idols, making their eyes bigger, their nose smaller and their skin brighter, and all for social media likes. It's just another reason why we are living in a world of FOMO,[1] sadness, increased anxiety, and Snapchat dysmorphia. It's time to acknowledge the damaging effects that social media [have] on people's self-image.[2]

We've seen that Song of Songs is a series of love songs or poems in which a young woman and a young man speak to and about each other. It starts abruptly with a passionate expression of desire, as we saw a few chapters ago. In the next song, we find the young woman talking about her physical appearance and what people think of it. How contemporary can you get?

BBC reporter Alexandra Jones actually joined the self-beautifying experiment. Her article is called 'I tried "Instagram face" for a week and here's what happened . . .' with the strapline 'The rise of selfie make-up and our quest for hyper-perfection'. She writes:

> Even those who aren't plugged into beauty trends will have clocked the rise of the 'Insta baddie', a look pioneered by the

likes of Kim Kardashian. The look – which is defined by fuller lips, large, Kewpie-doll eyes, a slim nose and aristocratic cheekbones – is one that the most popular Snapchat lenses, like the pink furry ears (you know which ones) and the dog filter, favoured by celebrities like Ariana Grande, mimic. Together they've helped create a new beauty ideal that – in totally expected news – experts say is almost impossible to come by naturally. The next day I feel bouncy from the reaction The Face has gotten on the 'gram – more than a hundred likes, so many comments of praise. Fire emojis, 'you look amazings', and almost 20 new followers. All from one picture.[3]

Does my face look good in this?

Social media have intensified an age-old insecurity in both women and men about their appearance. In the second movement of the Song we find a young woman being defiant about her appearance even though it does not conform to societal beauty stereotypes:

Song 1:5   Dark am I, yet lovely,
            daughters of Jerusalem,
            dark like the tents of Kedar,
            like the tent curtains of Solomon.
Song 1:6   Do not stare at me because I am dark,
            because I am darkened by the sun.
            My mother's sons were angry with me
            and made me take care of the vineyards;
            my own vineyard I had to neglect.

She has skin which has been made very dark by exposure to the sun. We may think that that is exactly what we would love, but in her society it meant the person was a farm labourer. The models and princesses had light skin. She explains that she has been forced to work in the family vineyard. Her father does not seem to have been alive, or able to stand up for her against the authoritarian behaviour of her brothers who have exploited her like a servant. It has left her vulnerable to feeling that she will not find a husband because she doesn't have the prized pale skin. In our society the equivalent would be a woman who feels insecure about her chest size or a man about his abs.

Beyond photo sharing

However, the young woman in the Song does have a lover who sees beyond socially determined stereotypes. He says to her:

> How beautiful you are, my darling!
> Oh, how beautiful!
> (Song 1:15)

This is what each of us longs for, isn't it? It is not hard to perceive a human application that pushes us beyond socially constructed, media-driven stereotypes to see real beauty in someone else and to tell him or her. The key is to allow God to reveal to us the unique physical beauty in another person, and allow that to shape our standard of beauty. The result is that that person's appearance now defines what we regard as beautiful.[4] So, if she is small-breasted, that is your definition of beauty. If he has blue eyes, blue eyes are beautiful, and so on.

Can I believe it?

Yet, for all his protestations, the young woman is not quite sure if her lover really means it. She protests:

> I am a rose of Sharon,
> a lily of the valleys.
> (Song 2:1)

There were lots and lots of 'roses' and 'lilies'[5] in springtime in the Promised Land. The rains drenched the ground, which became carpeted with spring flowers – many thousands, perhaps millions of them. So she is saying, 'I am just an ordinary lily. I don't stand out from the crowd.' But he insists that she does:

> Like a lily among thorns
>   is my darling among the young women.
> (Song 2:2)

To him, she is the most beautiful woman on earth.

How does this apply to our relationship with Christ? We have thought about how desirable our souls should and do find Jesus (Song 1:2). But this is about the *Lover's* pleasure in the *beloved's* beauty. In the normal way we interpret the metaphor, that ought to translate to *Christ's* pleasure in *our* beauty. At which point, most Christian readers who are well schooled in the biblical theology of human sin will ask, 'What?!'

Christ is not drawn to us because of anything beautiful in us. Naturally, we are spiritually dead (Ephesians 2:1), and we are willingly led by desires that are focused on the wrong things, which we gratify selfishly, and so we deserve not God's appreciation but his judicial wrath (Ephesians 2:3). We have nothing in us to make him desire us. But his love is undeserved, unmerited, uncalled for, unexpected and transforming. That is amazing, and it's the meaning of grace.

Contagious beauty

There is a character in Don Winslow's novel *The Power of the Dog* who is all too aware of the ugliness of his life, and finds himself hoping that a relationship with a woman might change that by transferring her moral beauty to himself:

> Callan remembers the girl he saw there, Nora. Remembers how much he wanted that girl, and how Big Peaches took her away from him. He remembers how beautiful she was, and thinking that if he could somehow touch that beauty, it would make his own life less ugly. But that was a long time ago . . .

and it's not possible that the girl Nora is still in that house.
Is it?[6]

That is a surprisingly accurate image of what happens in the gospel.
Martin Luther, pioneer of the Protestant Reformation, pictures
God's grace coming to us to see what it can find: 'The grace of God
does not find . . . that which is pleasing to it.'[7]

How does it work?

The Song of Songs does not contradict this foundational biblical
teaching. But that still does not solve our problem with this text.
How can we read this assertion by the young woman that she is
beautiful as being about our souls? How can we understand the
man's emphatic corroboration of what she says – 'How beautiful you
are, my darling! Oh, how beautiful!' – as being about us?

When we see the beauty of Christ, we become aware of our own
natural spiritual and moral ugliness. It is dismaying. It crushes our
illusions. The false view we have of our own moral attractiveness is
shattered, devastatingly. It is a view that we have painstakingly
constructed for ourselves – and for others. It makes us feel safe. But
it is brittle and false. And when we see the beauty of Christ, it shrivels
and melts, leaving us naked and embarrassed.

This would be like a man who prided himself on his finely
chiselled abdominal muscles looking down to see that he has been
kidding himself, and actually there is a grotesquely bulging pot belly,
not the result of some unfortunate problem with metabolizing food
but entirely his own overeating. Or it would be like a woman who
faced the world day by day confident in her own beautifully clear
skin, looking in the mirror and finding that the mirror was lying
and actually she had oozing pustules all over her face.

Looking up

However, when we have seen our own spiritual ugliness, something
unexpected happens, if we will only let it. We look up, thinking that

anyone who sees us as we really are will avert his or her gaze and cross the road to avoid us, but we find an extraordinary sight awaiting us: Christ in all his beauty is walking towards us.

When we feel at our most ugly, with torn, foul-smelling clothes and repulsive contortions to our faces, like people who have been cruel all their lives, we see him running in our direction. He is moving towards us, smiling, and calling as soon as we are within earshot, 'I've come to make you beautiful. Let's start with those rags.'

From the bag he is carrying he brings out a set of clean bright clothes, helps us off with ours and on with his. Our old disgusting clothes seem to vanish. Then in the distance we can see through a tunnel down through time to a hill. On the hill we can make out a man hanging on a criss-cross pole. As we look closer, we see he is wearing clothes that look and smell, even at a distance, remarkably like the ones we have just taken off. Amazing!

Now look in the mirror

Now we are in a position to do something even more remarkable – to find that we look in the mirror and see something new. We no longer see the false self, and appreciate properly the beauty of what we are in Christ. Christ is 'our righteousness', writes Paul in 1 Corinthians 1:30. We could equally translate this as: Christ is 'our justification'. The point is amplified in Galatians 2:15–16. (To make this passage a little clearer, I have inserted my own comments in brackets into Paul's words below.)

> We who are Jews by birth and not sinful Gentiles [Paul means Jews who understand the Old Testament properly] know that a person is not justified by the works of the law [many Jews thought this, but they were reading the Old Testament wrongly; self-justification is impossible, whether we try to compensate for our failings by keeping God's standards or even our own], but by faith in Jesus Christ. [Self-justification is impossible, but trusting in Jesus does make us right with God.]

This truth is confirmed in the next sentence:

> So we, too, have put our faith in Christ Jesus that we may be justified by faith in Christ and not by the works of the law, because by the works of the law no one will be justified.

Negatively, this means that we contribute nothing to being put right with God. Positively, it means that in Christ God puts us in the right, in the clear, with himself. As he assesses our moral worth, he does not now look at us and see us as disobedient, rebellious, disloyal, dirty people who have harmed others rather than caring for them, who have cheated or discriminated against others rather than treating them fairly, who have exerted power over others in wrong ways, and above all have failed to love God as we should. He no longer sees us that way. Instead, it is as if he sees all of that (real though it is) as cloaked, covered over and replaced with the perfect moral goodness of Christ.

Cloaked and covered

Let's pick up that clothing imagery. Naturally, we are the people of Isaiah 64:6:

> All of us have become like one who is unclean,
>   and all our righteous acts are like filthy rags . . .

But in the gospel God gives us a different set of clothes – Jesus' clothes. This is pictured most graphically in Zechariah 3:

> Then he showed me Joshua the high priest standing before the angel of the LORD, and Satan standing at his right side to accuse him. The LORD said to Satan, 'The LORD rebuke you, Satan! The LORD, who has chosen Jerusalem, rebuke you! Is not this man a burning stick snatched from the fire?'
>   Now Joshua was dressed in filthy clothes as he stood before the angel. The angel said to those who were standing before him, 'Take off his filthy clothes.'

Then he said to Joshua, 'See, I have taken away your sin, and I will put fine garments on you.'

Then I said, 'Put a clean turban on his head.' So they put a clean turban on his head and clothed him, while the angel of the LORD stood by.

(Zechariah 3:1–5)

Undeserved purity

Martin Luther loved this picture of pure clothing and called it Christ's 'alien righteousness'. He meant that it comes from a different world, as though from spiritual outer space. It is not from the moral world of our own lives, because we cannot weave together that kind of cloak or purify ourselves. But it comes from the outside, and is given to us to put on, covering over and replacing our guilt in God's sight.

That is now how God sees us. Perfect, pure, clean, good, loyal, fair, just, loving, obedient, law-keeping. Christ's record is now our record. And God sees that as beautiful. Christ himself looks on *us* and sees *his* beauty.

The creation of beauty

Luther loved this and built his whole life on it. What makes this all the more remarkable is how much Luther loathed his sin and feared God's judgment. Over time he came to understand the beauty of God's grace properly. What Luther actually wrote in the quote earlier, included two words which I rather mischievously left out.

I quoted: 'The grace of God does not find . . . that which is pleasing to it.' But actually he wrote: 'The grace of God does not find *but creates* that which is pleasing to it.'

There are rich dimensions to this. As we look at different parts of the Song, we will explore them more fully. For now, though, I invite you to see yourself as Christ sees you – a justified sinner, simultaneously one who deserves to be punished for your moral ugliness and one who is also unpunished, accepted and delighted in because he has wrapped his moral beauty around you.

A picture in the loft?

A friend of mine doesn't look much older at forty-two than he did at twenty-two (lucky man!). Another friend says affectionately, 'He must have a picture in the loft.' This is a reference to Oscar Wilde's novel, *The Portrait of Dorian Gray*. Dorian is a highly attractive-looking man who goes through life behaving selfishly and cruelly but seems to get more and more handsome as the years go by. In the magic fairy-tale logic of the story, the loft of his house contains a painting of Dorian. As time unfolds, the face in the portrait ages and becomes more and more cruel and ugly. It reflects the person he is becoming.

In the gospel, in a sense, a similar thing happened to Jesus. It is as if all our ugliness has been transferred to him once for all on the cross, where he was 'made . . . to be sin for us' (2 Corinthians 5:21) and 'his appearance was so disfigured beyond that of any human being and his form marred beyond human likeness' (Isaiah 52:14) that he looked 'appalling'. The former is a verse that destroys one world and builds another. It means that Christ now looks on us with delight, because he sees his own beauty – and he loves it.

In the words of the lover in the Song, Christ says to us, 'How beautiful you are, my darling! Oh, how beautiful!'

A big surprise

As I have explained the Song, this is one of the things that is most surprising and unexpected to my hearers. They find it quite hard to believe it, and to hear Christ's words. They are so convinced of their own unrighteousness and 'unbeauty' that it just seems wrong. But over time, as they understand justification better and see the link with the idea of beauty in the Song, the Holy Spirit enables them to believe that this is true and to hear Jesus saying it to them. And it is what we all need too. As Strachan and Sweeny put it:

> More than repaired self-esteem, more than pain-free lives, more than anything we can imagine, we need more of God, more of

His peace, more of His joy – in order that we, growing more beautiful, might give Him more of the glory that He, being beauty itself, deserves.[8]

Others may criticize us or judge us. It may be justified criticism, or criticism based on the subjective standards of society like that of the people looking down on the young woman in the Song for being excessively sun-kissed. We may judge ourselves similarly, by God's standards, by our own standards, by others' standards.

But I don't want to look inside

We find it hard to look deep into ourselves, and we fear anyone else doing the same. Worst of all would be for God to do that. In a chilling novel, *The Old Religion*, Martyn Waites creates a terrifying character called Morrigan, who manipulates and controls people. Another character in the book falls prey to this person and is filled with horror:

> How did Morrigan always do this to him? It was as though Morrigan had some kind of power, some method to look right inside him, find the part of him that was full of fears and self-pity, self-disgust and self-loathing, that cordoned-off area he didn't show to anyone, not even himself if he could help it, and rip it out for all to see? And he didn't know how it was done. If it was a mind trick then it was a damned good one. If [it] was some kind of witchcraft, then that really terrified him.[9]

We fear that God is like that. But in fact Morrigan is more like Satan. God does look right inside us, but he doesn't 'rip it all out for all to see' – he covers it with his Son's righteousness, as we saw earlier.

Fear of exposure

So many of us go through life like the person we met earlier in the song by The Killers – sick of the thought that people might be judging us, frightened of what they could find. The singer goes on to say that he feels he can just about cope with life as long as somebody takes him home occasionally.[10]

That is how so many of us deal with these insecurities, even though, ultimately, no human 'somebody' who takes us home is enough. But Christ is. He has taken us to his home; he has made our soul his home. In the infinity of his love, he is able to relate to each believer as if every one of us was special to him, beautiful in our own unique way.

How does this work?

Someone suggested an analogy which could help us to understand how this may work:

> I've noticed a mismatch between my perception of my wife's beauty and her own perception of her beauty. When she looks at herself in the mirror, she does so with a critical gaze. So, what she sees reflected back is that critical expression.
>
> But when I look at her, particularly in more intimate moments, she is smiling at me and everyone looks at their most attractive when they are smiling. What she sees when she sees herself is judgment. What I see when I see her is love.
>
> I wonder if this helps account for the delight Christ finds in us? When we look at ourselves, we see judgment. But when Christ looks at us, he sees love, a love evoked by his prior love. We look into his face and see a smile. In response, we smile. This is what Christ sees, and it is beautiful. And it really is beautiful. He's not just pretending to find us beautiful.[11]

Hearing his voice

The above idea hints at something that will challenge us even more (and take us possibly even higher) – the beauty of Christ which he progressively creates and appreciates, not simply around us but *in* us. But that belongs later. For now, I invite you to hear Christ speaking to you and saying:

Ah, you are beautiful, my love;
   ah, you are beautiful . . .
(Song 1:15 NRSV)[12]

Meditation

Take a moment to read this:

Ah, you are beautiful, my love;
   ah, you are beautiful.

Hear the voice of Jesus speaking to you in those words. If you find that difficult, notice what your difficulties are and offer them to him in prayer. You may also like to lay this sentence alongside what someone, or more than one person, has said to you in the context of a romantic relationship or marriage. Give thanks for that – and then realize that Jesus' words are even greater words. Or perhaps there are words that you wish someone had said to you but hasn't, either recently or ever. Offer up to him that sense of missing out. And hear his words like a great flood of love, filling that space.

Prayer

Lord, I confess to you my insecurity – about how I look, about what I have achieved and not achieved, about how I have behaved and not behaved, about how others see me or don't see me. Thank you that you see me as beautiful, in your beauty. Help me hear these words. Amen.

7

Delight: the power of beauty

You may enjoy cooking competitions on television, as I do. To see a large pool of initial contestants whittled down through round after round of demanding tasks, as some grow and learn and others panic or underperform, creates a compelling narrative. Then there is the repeated drama of watching them describe, prepare, cook, arrange and present plates of food – and that ever-so-tense moment as the judges peer at it, smell it and sample it, before delivering a verdict which will make or destroy a contestant's chances and morale.

But the frustration of watching cooking on television is that you can only see it. Viewers at home cannot touch, smell, taste or normally even hear it.

The relationship between two lovers is about more than remote seeing (or hearing, or reading, for that matter). Letters, photographs, texting, even live talking or video-chatting, are not the same as being with the other. The meaning of two people becoming 'one flesh' is that all the lover's senses are receptive to the delights of the other person.

Our relationship with Christ is one of deep delight in all he is and all we can experience of him. He is beautiful. In Song 1:15–16 (NRSV) we read a touching interchange. The young man says to the woman:

> Ah, you are beautiful, my love;
>> ah, you are beautiful;
>> your eyes are doves.

She replies in almost the same words:

> Ah, you are beautiful, my beloved,
>> truly lovely.[1]

The beauty of Christ

We will see the man's appreciation of the woman's beauty later, but let's start with her finding *him* beautiful. That is so human and so wonderful.

How can we apply this to Christ? Jesus is simply beautiful. You may be wondering: where does it say that? We could point to the beauty of the Lord, which is revealed in the temple:

> One thing I ask from the LORD,
>   this only do I seek:
> that I may dwell in the house of the LORD
>   all the days of my life,
> to gaze on the beauty of the LORD
>   and to seek him in his temple.
> (Psalm 27:4)

We might stumble on a rather neglected promise in Isaiah 33:

> Your eyes will see the king in his beauty
>   and view a land that stretches afar.
> (Isaiah 33:17)

'Glorious' means 'beautiful'

I have found it helpful to realize that in the Bible the words 'glory' and 'beauty' are used in overlapping ways. Think of how often God is described as glorious. It's a word designed to make us admire him and delight in his beauty.

It is not physical beauty, because (1) God has no physical being and (2) Jesus himself was nothing special to look at, according to Isaiah 53:2.

How Jesus is beautiful

I am sure his smile was sweet and melting, but the point is that when we talk of Jesus' beauty, it is not physical beauty that we are thinking of, but the moral beauty of a pure, perfectly loving life. That is the glory of the Lord, revealed in the incarnation: 'the glory of the one and only Son, who came from the Father, full of grace and truth' (John 1:14). And also revealed on the cross (John 17:1).

Jesus' glory is beautiful – his holiness, his purity, his grace, his work of our salvation. The glorious beauty – or beautiful glory – of God is revealed to us in Christ. As Paul puts it: 'the light of the knowledge of God's glory [is] displayed in the face of Christ' (2 Corinthians 4:6).

Dane Ortlund summarizes it thus: 'The holy is the beautiful.'[2] In his most helpful book, Ortlund explains how the beauty of the Lord was at the centre of Jonathan Edwards' understanding of God, the gospel and the Christian life: 'The Christian life, [Edwards] says, is to enjoy and reflect the beauty of God. Christ, supremely in his mercy to sinners . . . is the magnetic beauty to which we are drawn.'[3]

The words of the woman in the Song are our words in response to the beauty of Christ: we say with her, 'Ah, you are beautiful, my beloved, truly lovely.'

The Song of Songs follows the pattern that we find elsewhere in the Bible of using images that appeal to our senses in the natural world to show us how Christ is beautiful.

Dreaming of love

The Song presents a rather dream-like sequence at the start of chapter 2, in which the woman fantasizes about her lover. She does so in sensory images. These remind her of what he could be to her – not remotely, like a well-cooked, beautifully presented dish on a television screen, but in close physical presence. The images speak to us of what Christ is to us:

Like an apple tree among the trees of the forest
  is my beloved among the young men.
(Song 2:3a)

Her lover is better than all the rest: Christ stands out from all other beauty and delight. He offers something that we cannot find elsewhere.

A thought experiment

Imagine yourself walking through a huge forest. We don't have any of those in the UK any more, so unless your country does, you may need to transport yourself to a different place or a different time, or both. You have been travelling for days. The forest is dark and oppressive. You have lost your way, and you have a horrible feeling that you may be going around in circles, but you can't even be sure about that. Your food is almost gone, and what is left is dull and tasteless. You have only brackish water from pools to drink. You feel happier out in the clearings that appear from time to time, but the sun is so hot that you have to keep retreating to the thick thorny undergrowth to escape it.

Then you come across a clearing, on the other side of which you can see a different kind of tree. There, red fruits are growing. You sprint across the clearing, through the hot sun, and arrive panting at what you can now see is an apple tree. You flop exhausted in its shade and find a newly fallen red apple which you press to your mouth. Your teeth sink into the firm flesh and release streams of delicious juice.

You know how the woman feels as she talks about her lover:

I delight to sit in his shade,
    and his fruit is sweet to my taste.
(Song 2:3b)

The cooling shade

The pair of images used in the above quote evoke security and refreshment. Shade matters hugely in the Middle East in the summer. Increasingly, it matters in the UK too. In July 2019 a new record was set for the highest temperature ever recorded in the UK – in Cambridge, where I live.

Christ is the shade we need against the heat of the harsh sun of life. He protects us from being burned, and he brings down our core temperature to manageable levels. As we shelter under his canopy, we are secure. He has promised to provide for our needs (Luke 12:30–31). He will not allow anything to happen to us that is not part of his plan eventually to give us more of himself and all his gifts.

And as we shelter under his canopy, we find refreshment. He is the one who restores and refreshes our souls (Psalm 23:2–3). Think about the apple image for a moment. It conveys the need we have actually to reach out and take from the Lord what he wants to give us – to sink our teeth into his promises and extract the sweet juice and allow our souls to experience delight. What is that sweetness? The love of one who has done everything to save us from our sin and secure eternal life for us.

Come to the banquet

In her dream the woman then imagines herself being treated as an honoured guest at the home of some important figure, perhaps even a prince or a king:

Let him lead me to the banquet hall,
    and let his banner over me be love.
(Song 2:4)

Can you hear her desire? Do you sense the Holy Spirit replacing your desires for other things as you read this and realize this is where your soul will find its greatest delight, under a banner that says 'I love you'?

The picture of a banqueting hall is a rich one. Christ has done more than save us – he lives with us.

For the young woman in the Song, this is very much about a crazy longing that, itself, leaves her exhausted by its ferocity:

Strengthen me with raisins,
    refresh me with apples,
      for I am faint with love.
(Song 2:5)

Unsatisfied

Life is full of experiences that exhaust us with unsatisfied desire. We are driven to fill ourselves with the good things of this world, but they simply leave us needing God all the more. As they turn out to be unsatisfying, we find ourselves longing for more, not always realizing that it is Christ we are missing, but experiencing the craziness of desire to fill that space with love. That longing is a longing for the strengthening and refreshing that only Christ can bring. Every single earthly disappointment presses us towards him.

The woman continues to imagine (or dream of) closeness to her lover:

His left arm is under my head,
and his right arm embraces me.
(Song 2:6)

We have moved from the dining room to the bedroom. It is a picture of physical intimacy: he is caressing her. The human soul is programmed to long for the caresses of Christ. We seek soothing elsewhere, but no one soothes like Christ.

The early Puritan writer John Owen (1616–83) expounds on this. Christ is:

Lovely in his person, lovely in his birth, and Incarnation, lovely in the whole course of his life, lovely in his Death, lovely in his whole employment, lovely in the glory and majesty, lovely in all these supplies of Grace, lovely in all the tender Care, Power and Wisdom, lovely in all his Ordinances [that is, in the means of grace in the church – worship, preaching, prayer, communion, baptism, and so on], lovely and glorious in the vengeance he takes, lovely in the pardon he has purchased, altogether lovely.[4]

This is the one whose Spirit caresses your soul. Think about it!

Standing back

Let's stand back now and think about this section as a whole. It is highly charged, even erotic. It is *entirely natural* to feel ourselves wanting a *human* lover. If you are married, your mind should go to your husband or wife – but you may find stray thoughts popping up that make you ashamed. If you were married once, you may have a wrenching longing for an earlier stage in your life. If you are not married, you may find this quite a mixed experience, pointing you to something that God has not given you. The writer of the Song is well aware of what will happen to the reader, so he or she has something important to add:

> Daughters of Jerusalem, I charge you
> by the gazelles and by the does of the field:
> do not arouse or awaken love
> until it so desires.
> (Song 2:7)

Although what you are reading is a book about spiritual intimacy, not about sexuality, the two intermingle in the Song of Songs and in life, and therefore we cannot ignore what may happen to us as we read the Song and the warnings it contains (as well as the promises that sit alongside them).

Controlling our imagination and the danger of desire

The woman's fantasy or dream is in danger of taking her too far in her mind. She needs to take control of it and keep it within God-given boundaries. For a couple in a pre-marriage relationship this requires special effort. For an engaged couple there will be a natural anticipation of what will be right from the wedding day onwards, but for them to linger too long in their minds on that anticipation is only going to cause them difficulties. For unmarried people, this is an area that takes much learning and pain: what do I do with my desires, which are not even partially fulfilled?

Modern society teaches us to follow the advice of the eighteenth-century poet and painter William Blake, that we should 'sooner murder an infant in its cradle than nurse unacted desires'.[5] In other words, to repress desire is about the worst thing you can do, worse even than murdering a baby. In fact, he sees our desires as little beings that need to be allowed to grow and develop, and find their consummation in whatever it is they are focused on.

God's word to us, by contrast, is very different: keep desire under control. Take all the steps you need not to awaken it prematurely – not simply through willpower and an effort to be obedient, but through seeking all the satisfaction you can have in Christ in this life. Pastor and author Philip Ryken explains this well:

> When it comes to our sexuality, [God] doesn't want us to settle for smaller pleasures that surely will get in the way of greater satisfaction. This might include having a marriage that lasts, but more importantly, it definitely includes the deep joy of having a closer relationship with him, whether we are married or single. Sexual restraint is spiritually fruitful. One day the cross-bearing we do with our sexual desires will be crowned with honour and consummated in the eternal love of Jesus Christ. The reason God tells us not to awaken sexual desire before its time is very simple: when we share sexual intimacy with the wrong person at the wrong time – or when we gratify sexual desire all by ourselves – we destroy relationships.[6]

We are wired for intimacy. We seek it elsewhere, in both the wrong and the right places. But all those longings and all those experiences are designed to propel us towards Christ – the disappointments, because he will not disappoint; the satisfactions, because they are only ever partially satisfying and Christ is more satisfying. He is the Lover of our souls, and he makes us more secure and more refreshed than anything or anyone else.

Being close to Jesus

Remember the hymn from which this book got its title: 'Jesus, Lover of my soul, let me to thy bosom fly'? We noted earlier that the first line is odd to sing, and the second line odder still! It may help us to realize that in older forms of English the meaning of the word 'bosom' used to include a man's chest, as in the account of the Last Supper in the Authorized (King James) Version, which says: 'Now there was leaning on Jesus' bosom one of his disciples, whom Jesus loved' (John 13:23). Other translations say: 'was reclining *next* to him' (NIV), or 'was reclining at table at Jesus' *side*' (ESV). If you do a little search with some Bible software, you will find that 'at his side' or 'on his bosom' only appears in one other place in John's Gospel, in 1:18:

> No one has ever seen God; the only God, *who is at the Father's side*, he has made him known.
> (ESV)

> No man hath seen God at any time; the only begotten Son, *which is in the bosom of the Father*, he hath declared him.
> (KJV)[7]

What Charles Wesley did was to pick up the language of the relationship within the Trinity from John 1 and link it to the special relationship with John the beloved disciple. Then, in a daring but entirely justified move, he made it his prayer for himself and for all who sing his hymn.

We long to be as close to Jesus as he is to his Father, and as John, his especially beloved disciple, was to Jesus at the Last Supper. We do not have to envy John. We can be where he was. As Jesus says later in John's account of the Last Supper: 'You will realise that I am in my Father, and you are in me, and I am in you' (John 14:20).

That occasion of the Last Supper was where Jesus gave us a pattern of remembering his love and enjoying it in a special way. The bread and wine of the church's celebration of the Lord's Supper provide tangible and powerful symbols of Christ's love for us. They are a foretaste of a wedding feast, the final, ultimate and endless Lord's Supper of his return. As we eat the bread, the very acts of tasting, chewing, swallowing and digesting speak to our souls of our union with him – he is in us and we are in him. The sensation of the wine (or grape juice) sliding over our tongues and slipping down our throats draws us deeper into this intimacy. A communion service is not simply about remembering his love, but also about enjoying it in the moment and savouring the lingering flavour of being united with Jesus.[8]

Questions

Dwell on one of the images we have discussed in this chapter for a few minutes before you move on.

- How does the idea of Christ as a shady canopy or a sweet fruit, or whatever the image may be, move you?
- How does it connect with what is going on in your life right now?

Prayer

Lord, I bring myself and all my needs and longings to you. I confess that I am not strong at controlling my desires or seeing how they are met directly or indirectly in you. But thank you for these powerful pictures of you as my security, my protection, my refreshment, my pleasure. Amen.

8

Springtime: when fancy turns to love

He hesitated, his hand holding the telephone, but his fingers not quite ready to dial the number. A hundred cautious thoughts surged through his mind. Can I? Should I? Dare I? What if she says no? What if I get her housemate? What if she laughs? What if I get hurt, again?

Then he thought of her hair, chestnut-red, tumbling in gloriously untidy curls down over her shoulders. He remembered that smile and the sparks that seemed to fly when they made eye contact across the group drinking coffee after church.

Something tensed in his stomach, gripping him with a feeling like a surge of water towards a dam. The dam burst. He dialled the number.

'Hi. What are you doing on Saturday? I'd like to drive over to Cardiff and take you out to lunch.'

Slight pause.

'OK,' she replied.[1]

Making the first move

All relationships start with someone making a movement towards someone else. Someone has to take the initiative. That includes our relationship with Christ. Naturally, we are spiritually dead and we will never seek after him (Ephesians 2:1–3), so he has to come to find us. Driving all the way from Aylesbury to Cardiff (only about 130 miles but a bit of an effort as a day trip there and back) seemed no effort at all to me if 'she' would let me take her out to lunch. But in his love Christ comes to find us, and embarks on a journey from eternity into history, from infinity into humanity, from heaven to a manger, a workshop, a cross and a tomb.

In chapter 2 of the Song of Songs we find a beautiful poem which describes the movement of the lover towards his beloved, portraying for us the movement of Christ towards our souls. We hear it from the woman's perspective:

Listen! My beloved!
Look! Here he comes . . .
(Song 2:8)

She hears and sees him. This is what happens as our souls come alive to what Christ has done for us. An awareness grows that, far from staying at a distance, or moving further away as our sin builds and builds, he is moving towards us. He has done so in his own earthly history – the incarnation. And he does so dynamically in our own earthly history as his Spirit opens our eyes to the gospel.

In the Song, the woman portrays the movement of her lover as that of a gazelle on rocky outcrops (2:8b–9a). Mountain deer are astonishingly agile creatures – and graceful with it. They spring effortlessly over broken, rock-strewn slopes that even the most athletic human would have to navigate cautiously. Her lover moves like a ballet dancer combined with a fell runner, driven by the joys of spring and a desire to be near her.

This is Christ's movement towards our souls. It is highly energetic, driven by a deep-seated longing that impels him forward. His joy at the thought of coming closer makes him spring and bound over any obstacle. Think of the energy of a deer moving down a steep hillside: that is Christ's energy as he comes towards you.

The woman portrays the deer as coming right up to her family home:

Look! There he stands behind our wall,
gazing through the windows,
peering through the lattice.
(Song 2:9b)

Apparently, deer that live in forests close to inhabited areas do behave like this! For this woman, it signifies his eagerness to be near her. Spiritually, it points to how eager Christ is to come near to us. He longs to be close to us and have a relationship with us.

Great expectations?

Christ moved towards us in the incarnation. Now, by his Spirit, he is in constant motion in our souls. What a vital thing to realize about Jesus as the Lover of our souls! He is constantly dancing down the mountain, moving across the fields, looking in through the window of our souls into the depths of who we are.

The question is: what does he expect and want to find? Does he peer into our souls hoping to find an inner life as beautiful and ordered as his own? We might well think so; surely he would want a soul to match his own soul, full of love and virtue.

That is a natural assumption, but it is wrong. Christ is wise enough not to expect it on his approach to us, and to know that he would be disappointed if he did! He knows the strange mixture of dignity and disorder that lives inside us. He sees fully that if our lives were houses, they might look well decorated on the outside, but inside they are as messy as a teenager's bedroom.

So, what is Jesus looking for? What does he desire? Surely this: a heart that knows it needs him and is ready to receive him. Isaiah writes about the two places where God dwells:

> I live in a high and holy place,
>   but also with the one who is [broken] and lowly in spirit,
> to revive the spirit of the lowly
>   and to revive the heart of the [broken].
> (Isaiah 57:15b)[2]

The significance is massive. Christ bounds towards us and peers into our souls, wanting to find us so broken by sin that we have space for him to come in and bring new life.[3] At the conscious level, we therefore ask ourselves, 'Am I broken? Great! Can I do anything about it? No? Even better.' That's what Jesus is looking for. That means there is space for him!

OK to be broken

We should add that if someone is conscious of being broken, hopeless and open to outside help at an even deeper level, the Holy Spirit has entered and done that work of brokenness. He is the one who breaks us. We acknowledge the brokenness and open ourselves to Christ's gaze. You say: what about my sin? Dane Ortlund explains this helpfully: 'It is not the absence of sin that is the key mark of regeneration but the hatred of it.'[4] He comments that 'new birth grants a new direction, not a new perfection'.[5]

Your story

Are you a Christian? If so, this is for you, and this is your personal story. If you are not, think about this as a poetic description of the most important, most real thing that can ever happen to you. As you are reading this, Christ himself is moving towards you, accelerating in his eagerness to look into your soul and see space for himself.

And as he springs towards the beloved, the lover says, 'Look, it's spring!'

My beloved spoke and said to me,
   'Arise, my darling,
    my beautiful one, come with me.
See! The winter is past;
    the rains are over and gone.
Flowers appear on the earth;
    the season of singing has come,
the cooing of doves
    is heard in our land.
The fig-tree forms its early fruit;
    the blossoming vines spread their fragrance.'
(Song 2:10–13a)

It's springtime

This is Christ's invitation to us. As he speaks, the winter of our soul is coming to an end. It reminds me of the Beatles song 'Here Comes the Sun'.[6] Rather plaintively, it speaks of a long lonely winter and how it feels like ages have passed since the previous summer. Then the tone changes because the sun and spring are here. That is Christ speaking to your soul.

In the Middle East, rain really matters. Spring means that the parched ground has been well watered. Birds are singing their songs. Trees are starting to burst with fruit; flowers are releasing sweet smells. It is a total sensory experience of newness, freshness, life! For the man in the Song, it is a picture of all the relationship can be.

As we apply this to our souls, we hear Christ inviting us to live with him, to join him in a new life:

Arise, come, my darling;
    my beautiful one, come with me.
(Song 2:13b)

This is his voice to you. Will you let him lead you into the spring of new Christian life?

Yet, not everyone enjoys spring. T. S. Eliot wrote in his long poem 'The Waste Land' about how cruel a month April can be.[7] Florence Welch, in 'South London Forever', sings about a kind of sadness that she associates with springtime.[8] For them, the flowers and the bursting shoots and the new life and the frolicking lambs contrast horribly with the deadness and sadness of human souls.

Spring can mock us with its fertility and its promise, because our lives seem so different. Even the joyful energy of the human reading of Song 2:7–13 can mock us too, because once life felt like that, but now he or she is not here. But Christ comes to us. He keeps saying, 'Arise, come, my darling; my beautiful one, come with me.'

He is moving towards us, even if it feels as though no one else is.

It would be easy to leave the application there, and not to develop it beyond the initial movement of Christ calling us to follow him, covered already with the beauty of his righteousness. But that would be to undersell what this text offers us.

A dynamic relationship

In a profound piece of pastoral analysis, in his work on the Song, Richard Sibbes suggests we find in it both Christ's initial move towards us and his future final move towards us when he returns. But Christ also comes to us in a whole series of 'intermediate comings'.[9] What Sibbes means is that our relationship with Christ is not static but dynamic. He is constantly moving towards us, drawing near, peering inside, looking to see if the beauty he desires is there: beauty of space for him, created by our brokenness and sense of need, our willingness for him to be our Lover. Robert Jenson suggests that this is often a powerful experience:

> Where the Lord comes, in the reading of [the Word] or the celebration of Eucharist or in any of a hundred events of his 'real presence' among his people, something of the final and first-intended fulfillment opens to our experience; we are in the 'gate of heaven,' as Martin Luther described the church. We have one foot in perfected Eden. And there we are even now one with the Lord.[10]

Love is not static. And if it is, it is not love. The same is true of our relationship with Christ. He, of course, never changes in himself. But we change, and our experience of him changes as we change. We find even greater depths, fresh colour combinations, new tones in his voice. And he is constantly moving towards us saying, 'Arise, come, my darling; my beautiful one, come with me.'

Jeremy is a busy young professional who works with young adults. On hearing these reflections on the Song of Songs, he realized that:

> For the last couple of years I have been largely settling for getting through a half-hour quiet time each morning, when I will read a passage, perhaps a commentary on it, have a couple

of thoughts, and say a few prayers, while regularly getting distracted by thoughts about my work and not really having any sense of actively entering into the presence of Christ, his loving eyes on me, my opening myself to him and enjoying him, or really anything of this more genuinely relational nature. All of which is to say that I need this invitation to know Christ more deeply very much indeed.

What about you? Will you listen to his voice speaking to you? Will you let him lead you into spring again?

Questions

- How does this picture of the dynamism of Christ's movement towards you affect you?
- How is he speaking to you through these pictures right now?

Prayer

Lord Jesus Christ, thank you that you came bounding from the mountain of high heaven to the village of earth to live and die for me. Thank you that one day you will return. Thank you that you keep moving towards my soul and calling to me to come with you. Help me to discern your movements and respond to them. Amen.

9
Belonging: together, for ever

When Tigranes and his wife were both taken prisoners by Cyrus, Cyrus, turning to Tigranes, asked, 'What will you give for the liberation of your wife?' And the King answered, 'I love my wife, so that I would cheerfully give up my life if she might be delivered from servitude.' Whereupon Cyrus said that if there was such love as that between them, they might both go free.

So, when they were away, and many were talking about the beauty and generosity of Cyrus, and especially about the beauty of his person, Tigranes, turning to his wife, asked her what she thought of Cyrus, and she answered that she saw nothing anywhere but in the face of the man who had said that he would die if she might only be released from servitude. 'The beauty of that man,' she said, 'makes me forget all others.'

The preacher who used this illustration invited his hearers to follow suit: 'And verily we would say the same of Jesus.'[1] We are called to marital and spiritual monogamy!

This is the mutual possession within a covenant of non-equals that we find in the Song:

My beloved is mine and I am his;
    he browses among the lilies.
(Song 2:16)

Is monogamy dull?

A famous, talented and successful film actress announced that monogamy is rather dull and maybe even mad. She had a more 'sensible' arrangement:

She lives in a large, rambling house in Scotland with her twins and their father – and her lover, a beautiful, shaggy-haired artist nearly twenty years younger than she is, sometimes lives there too. When pressed by reporters, she has called her arrangement 'sane', which is about the last word most of us would associate with that kind of home life. 'We are all a family,' she has said. 'What you must also know is that we are all very happy.'[2]

The *Harper's Bazaar* (I am tempted to rewrite it as *Harper's Bizarre*) article concludes: 'It is an act of imagination to live differently from everyone else, and maybe, in rare and magnificent moments, it works.' Except that it appears that the first relationship ended in 2005 and the actress reverted to a monogamous life with the younger man. The 'sane arrangement' turned out not to be so sane after all.[3]

The biblical pattern for marriage is lifelong exclusiveness, particularly romantic and sexual exclusiveness. Not that there are no other relationships – of course there are (with children, parents, other family members, friends, colleagues and so on). But if you are married, your most important relationship is with your husband or wife.

Tied together

The Bible has different ways of speaking about this relationship. We think of Adam and Eve becoming 'one flesh' in Genesis 2:24, which introduces and summarizes the idea in the most pregnant of phrases. The idea of covenant as an unbreakable commitment takes us further and deeper. Sometimes people argue that polygamy is approved of in the Old Testament. However, the dysfunctional marriages and sexual sin that follow from Genesis 4 onwards actually portray every occasion of polygamy as ending badly.[4]

In the Song of Songs this commitment is expressed as mutual belonging. The idea is so important that it appears three times, in slightly different forms. The first is early on:

My beloved is mine and I am his;
>   he browses among the lilies.
(Song 2:16)

Total mutuality

Song 2:16 uses the language of mutual possession. It borrows a form of words from the covenant God made with Israel and applies it to human relationships. The spiritual reading of the Song borrows it back again for our relationship with Christ.

Christ has committed himself irrevocably to us. In a day when people prefer to say 'maybe' rather than 'yes' or 'no', this is a bit different. But that is what he has said and done. So, we can say, 'My beloved is mine.' He is our Saviour, our bread of life, our living water, our sacrifice, our atonement, our resurrected giver of new life. And of course, we belong to him too and have to adjust our lives accordingly.

In the Song, the wedding in chapters 3 and 4 is followed by an experience of marital night-time difficulties. Then there are songs of reconciliation, and towards the end of these the young woman repeats the mutual possession formula but now with the order reversed:

I am my beloved's and my beloved is mine;
>   he browses among the lilies.
(Song 6:3)

The change is marked and right. It is mutual possession, but it is not completely symmetrical. The most important thing is that I belong to Jesus. It takes priority because he is Lord.

Putting him first

We need to lay this alongside all the competition for the prime place in our lives. Anything that is more important to us than Jesus is an idol, sitting on the throne that belongs to him. When we become

Christians, we ask him to sit on that throne, but it is not a once-for-all movement psychologically. It is one we have to repeat regularly through our Christian lives. Our hearts feel the pull of other masters, other beauties, and other things which will, they whisper, satisfy us even more than Jesus.

This repeated pattern of dethroning idols needs more than determination or remorse. It needs divine power, but that is what Christ's passion, his exclusive commitment to us, gives us.

Towards the end of the Song of Songs, as the lovers reflect on their marriage, she remarks on the power of his feelings for her:

> I belong to my beloved,
>   and his desire is for me.
> (Song 7:10)

The power of desire

That word 'desire' is found only three times in the Old Testament: here, in Genesis 3:16: 'Your desire will be for your husband, and he will rule over you', and in Genesis 4:7: 'If you do not do what is right, sin is crouching at your door; it desires to have you, but you must rule over it.'

This background helps us to see the significance of Song 7:10. The language of mutual possession can too easily be received in a rather static way. Of course, it is meant to give us a sense of security like a wall that cannot be breached or a solid foundation built on to flawless granite substrate. But Song 7:10 points to the dynamic of desire within the mutual possession. We could call it the dynamic of divine possessiveness.

The American theologian Ellen Davis puts it this way:

> The desire of the Divine Lover is also directed toward us. This is the good news: however eagerly sin lurks to catch us, God seeks us even more ardently. To the extent that we can receive and respond to God's burning desire for us, we shall indeed achieve mastery over sin.[5]

The mutual possession is just that, mutual, but it is not completely symmetrical. This is because there is a properly passionate possessiveness in Christ's heart which longs for us to reciprocate – and uses the fires of his desire in order to ignite in us the fires of desire that keep our hearts exclusively his.

Let us not forget that he is totally committed to us: 'My beloved is mine!' he says. We can say, 'Jesus is mine! He belongs to me and I belong to him. Nothing can tear me out of his grasp; nothing can loosen the grip of his love on my life. He has bought me. He owns me. I am his and he is mine.'

Unbreakable commitment

The 1960s hit record 'Will You Still Love Me Tomorrow?' was written by married couple Gerry Goffin and Carole King. It evokes with great tenderness the dilemma of a teenage *girl* whose boyfriend wants to sleep with her (perhaps for the first time?).

She is greatly drawn to him. She can see love shining in his eyes. She hears him saying she is the only one for him. There is sweetness in the way he gives his love. But a nagging feeling won't go away: will he still love her tomorrow? Is this just the pleasure of a moment or actually something precious that will last? Will her heart be broken the next day?[6]

In an age of free love, the girl's questions and doubts stand as a prophetic warning. Some of us will have been hurt by people who have broken promises to us, whether within romantic or sexual relationships or in other spheres of our lives (families, workplaces, friendships). Human beings find it hard to be reliable. Except for Jesus Christ.

We can be sure that Christ has given himself to us completely, sharing his love with us sweetly in moments of great pleasure – and that this is a *lasting* treasure. He will still be ours tomorrow and next year and for ever. He is ours and we are his. For ever.

Meditation

Read this poem/hymn by William Cowper (1731–1800).

Hark, my soul, it is the Lord!
'Tis thy Saviour, hear His Word;
Jesus speaks, and speaks to thee,
'Say, poor sinner, lovest thou Me?

'I delivered thee when bound,
And, when bleeding, healed thy wound;
Sought thee wandering, set thee right,
Turned thy darkness into light.

'Can a woman's tender care
Cease toward the child she bare?
Yes, she may forgetful be,
Yet will I remember thee.

'Mine is an unchanging love,
Higher than the heights above,
Deeper than the depths beneath,
Free and faithful, strong as death.

'Thou shalt see My glory soon,
When the work of grace is done;
Partner of My throne shalt be:
Say, poor sinner, lovest thou Me?'

How will you reply? Can you just say, 'Yes, of course I do love you, Lord'? If so, that is wonderful; he has done a significant work in your heart to bring you to that place of instinctive affirmation. Lots of us, though, hesitate. Cowper himself, who suffered from depression, was like that. But he pondered Christ's question, and replied to it like this:

Lord, it is my chief complaint
That my love is weak and faint;
Yet I love Thee, and adore:
Oh for grace to love Thee more![7]

Say that to Jesus, out loud if possible. Why not try putting it in your own words, maybe writing it out?

10

Distance: we've lost that loving feeling

Jenny was waiting, the dinner simmering nicely on the stove top. It was her turn to cook on Wednesdays, Thursdays and Saturdays, something she and Jim had worked out in these early weeks of marriage. She had left work on time, made the easy commute home and started preparing food.

The key turned in the lock rather later than she had expected and Jim strode in, walked past her and headed upstairs to change. When he came down, she felt that she looked lovely, but his lack of reaction implied that something was not quite right.

'Hi, darling, dinner's ready,' she said cheerfully.

'Great, I'm starving,' he replied.

The food went down quickly, but Jim's attention was mostly on the TV across the room.

He did wash up but spent the evening on his phone, so that by bedtime Jenny realized they had had almost no eye contact over the last three hours. He went straight off to sleep. Jenny was left feeling that while she was close to him in physical proximity, emotionally she was deserted. She was at a bit of a loss to know what to do about the distance between them.

We can experience distance in our relationship with God too, and this can vary a good bit. When my father retired, my parents moved back to Devon where they had met and always wanted to live. They bought a lovely house with a sea view. We so enjoyed visiting them, but we often remarked on the weather, because in Dawlish it never seemed to stay still. We used to joke that you could get up for breakfast and by lunchtime have experienced four quite distinct conditions – sea fog, sunshine, a quick shower and a bright but overcast sky. The weather was highly variable.

There is a variability in human relationships too, and part of the way things vary is that sometimes we feel closer to someone we love and sometimes things feel more distant. As we keep seeing, relationships are not static, unlike two books next to each other on a shelf which may sit there for years cover to cover. Human relationships are more like grains of sand on a beach: close at one moment – and then a wave or a tide separates them.

You're not here!

Chapter 3 of the Song portrays the experience of distance:

> All night long on my bed
> > I looked for the one my heart loves;
> > I looked for him but did not find him.
> (Song 3:1)

If the man and woman are already married (which I doubt), she is literally in bed on her own. If they aren't, then this is some kind of nightmarish dream she is having; we may not necessarily take it literally, but it does portray a literal reality. Either way, she is saying 'Where are you?'

It comes as something of an unwelcome shock to Christians to realize that this is part of our experience of knowing Christ. We are like the woman who can't find her lover – where is he? The psalmist knew this feeling well:

> LORD, when you favoured me,
> > you made my royal mountain stand firm;
> but when you hid your face,
> > I was dismayed.
> (Psalm 30:7)

It feels as though Christ is a long way away. A missed promotion, a child's illness, an unanticipated expense that means a longed-for weekend break has to be abandoned: all manner of external disappointments can hit us harder than we expected and make us feel distant from God. Or a sense of flatness, emptiness or inner drag seems to flood our souls out of nowhere, leaving us with the sense that God is hiding somewhere behind a very distant planet.

Temporary desertion

The Puritan pastors of the sixteenth and seventeenth centuries observed this experience in their congregations and their own lives and pondered it deeply. They developed a label for it: 'spiritual desertion'.[1] That is the situation presented in Song 3:1. I wonder if you can identify with this too – the experience of saying to Christ, 'Where are you?'

What is immediately helpful about finding this in the Bible is that it says to us, 'You are not the first one to experience it, nor are you the only one.' This happens; it isn't nice (that's the point – as we will see), but it is a normal part of the Christian life, not something that has happened just to you and no one else.

If we are sensitive about our sin, we will probably assume that Christ has deserted us because of some pattern of sin that has grown up like bindweed in our life. That is a helpful assumption, because the Bible makes it clear that we can grieve the Spirit and make him withdraw from us. It is certainly what we find in Song 5:2–7 (as we will see in a later chapter).

Testing

However, not all spiritual desertions and experiences of God's absence are the direct result of sin. Something else may be happening. That seems to be the case in Song chapter 3: there is no hint that the lover is reacting to some fault in the beloved. We simply do not know the reason.

We get an example of this working in practice in the life of King Hezekiah in 2 Chronicles 32. First, the writer stresses how much God has blessed the king with 'very great wealth and honour' and how 'he succeeded in everything he undertook' (vv. 27, 30). Then a delegation comes from the east, and the writer lifts the curtain to explain what is happening behind the human scenes: 'But when envoys were sent by the rulers of Babylon to ask him about the miraculous sign that had occurred in the land, God left him to test him and to know everything that was in his heart' (v. 31).

God moves away. He withdraws his presence. The problem with being successful is that it is impossible without God's special help, but very often it is unclear just how much we have needed God's help to achieve that success: we tend to think it is just us. But without that help, we struggle.

That seems to have been what happened to Hezekiah. Without the presence of God, he made a mess of things with the Babylonian group, boasting about the treasures of the temple, even showing them off in person to the envoys, and thus setting things up for a return visit with muscle. Areas of weakness were revealed in his heart that he may not have realized were there.

It can be all too easy to think how strong we are when things are going well. Without God's special help, King Hezekiah found he couldn't stop himself showing off; he couldn't resist it, risky though it was. And then when the prophet Isaiah told him that it would end up in calamity for the nation, he resorted to the selfish comfort that things would be fine while *he* was alive (Isaiah 39).

A normal part of discipleship

The point is that God may choose to withdraw from us to put us to some kind of test. We may not like that, but we'd better accept it or we will struggle with this normal part of spiritual intimacy more than we need to. Take time to think about this in relation to the ups and downs of your own life.

In the Song the absence of the man is unexplained and painful, but the woman is determined to do something about it:

I will get up now and go about the city,
    through its streets and squares . . .
(Song 3:2a)

Fresh determination

Notice how determined the woman is. She is not going to let things rest. She is going to find her man, however tough that is, and going out at night in that culture was neither normal nor safe for a respectable female. The urban setting with its dangers pictures for us the effort we may need to make to restore relationships where there is unwanted distance. Am I going to accept that a friendship has gone cold? Will I let coolness towards my parents become permanent? Am I going to allow a temporary distance to become fixed like an unusually slow-drying super-adhesive, which is movable at first but gradually sets and goes rock hard?

In our relationship with Christ this is the response that the text draws us into – seeking him, doing what it takes to find him again. We listen to the woman's resolution: 'I will search for the one my heart loves' (Song 3:2b).

As the words echo in our souls, we find ourselves saying, 'Yes – I love him! I want him! I am going to search until I find him.'

Searching for Christ involves a number of things. We will want to do some self-analysis and ask if there is something we have done to offend him.[2] It may be simply that other things have absorbed us and we need to look away from them and talk to him. It may be that he has been testing us to see if we miss him or miss his help, and we need to see that both are true and turn back to him in appreciation.

Very often that is enough, and the sense of his presence is restored as he fills the space he left. But not always. The Song seems to portray a more protracted experience of Christ's absence in which it starts to feel as though he is deliberately avoiding us again and again.

When he seems evasive

Over the last three years I have grown a beard. That, combined with a few more grey hairs and some glasses with thick black rims, means that I look rather different from before. When I go to conferences, it feels as though I am in disguise. I arrived at one charity board meeting, only for the charity's National Director to wave at me politely, thinking that I was a guest speaker whom he had not met before. Spiritual desertion can feel as though Christ must be in disguise, because over a long period of time, even if we keep seeking him, we can't actually see him.

The young woman in the Song puts it very sadly: 'I looked for him but did not find him' (Song 3:2c). Many Christians know what this is like. Using the dream picture of being out at night (a dangerous thing), she imagines seeing people and asking them where her lover is – but they don't seem to know:

> The watchmen found me
> as they made their rounds in the city.
> 'Have you seen the one my heart loves?'
> (Song 3:3)

It is always good to ask others to help us 'find' Christ again, and very often hearing them reminding us of his grace is enough to restore it. In this case, though, it feels as if the watchmen are not much help, but then suddenly out of nowhere there he is again:

> Scarcely had I passed them
> when I found the one my heart loves.
> (Song 3:4a)

There is no rhyme nor reason; he is simply there, just as previously he wasn't there. She has not stopped seeking him – and finally he is there. That is how it feels sometimes.

You keep running away!

Our variable experience of Christ can be a bit like a playful child who keeps running away from us in a dark wood, and then coming back and then running away from us. Of course, eventually that becomes frustrating and annoying for an adult, especially if it feels as though it is time to go home. Christ's elusiveness can feel much less enjoyable than even that. But we need to persevere in seeking him, and keep deciding to give him the benefit of the doubt; he does know what he is doing and why.

Those are exceptionally important words for the Christian experiencing spiritual desertion. Charles Spurgeon, such a vibrant, larger-than-life character, knew this first-hand. In a powerful analysis of Spurgeon's struggles, Zack Eswine generalizes to the rest of us:

> At its core, spiritual depression concerns real or imagined desertions by God. We feel in our senses that He is angry with us, or we have done something to forfeit His love, or He has toyed with us and left us on a whim. Either way, He exists for others, but not for us. He punishes us with silent treatment. He laughs at our pain when He gossips to others about us.[3]

But the very presence of this experience in the life of Isaiah's hearers, a man like Spurgeon, and the soul in the spiritual reading of the Song, is reassuring: 'A larger story about God exists that possesses within it a language of sorrows, so that the gloomy, the anguished, the dark-pathed, and the inhabitants of deep night are given voice.'[4]

Think of your own experience of variability in your spiritual experience. There may be times when you know exactly why it has happened. There may be times when seeking Christ again quickly restores the relationship. But there may be times that are more puzzling. That makes the experience all the more difficult.

When it feels as if it's only me

In the third of his so-called gospel albums, *Shot of Love*, Bob Dylan sings about the variability of his relationship with Christ. As he walks through life, he can often hear footsteps, he says. When he turns around, sometimes someone is there; at other times it's only him.[5] None of us enjoys that feeling of being alone. It takes faith to believe that God still loves us. Isaiah says this is what we have to do:

Let the one who walks in the dark,
who has no light,
trust in the name of the LORD
and rely on their God.
(Isaiah 50:10)

What we can be sure of is that Christ knows precisely what he is doing, even if we don't and he doesn't show us. He has good purposes, even in the withdrawal of his light. As Iain Duguid suggests, God 'may withdraw the light of his presence for a while in order that I may see how dark or empty my life truly is without the joy of his salvation'.[6]

Lights back on

This truth may become clearer to us over time. As we decide to trust in Christ, we do start to 'find the One [our] heart loves'. We rediscover him:

Our sorrows belong to Jesus. He is their master, no matter what fiendish thought or unexplainable cause gave them birth. Jesus shows us His wounds, the slanders, the manipulations, the injustices, the body blows, the mistreatments piled on to Him. From there He loves, still. He invites us into fellowship with His empathy. We receive it from Him in the deeps.[7]

None of us finds spiritual desertion a welcome experience. But it is the way God characteristically works.

My ink-jet printer has a function called 'clean print head', which needs to be done from time to time. It has a deep-clean function too, which is done less often but goes deeper. If you feel deserted, it may well be because some sort of cleaning is going on. Ask God to make it a deep clean. The Lover of our souls sometimes needs to withdraw to remind our souls how much they want him. And then when you find him again, how much more tightly will you cling to him, echoing the woman in the Song: 'I held him and would not let him go' (Song 3:4b).

Questions

- How does this idea of spiritual desertion relate to your own experience as a Christian?
- Does it help you make sense of things that have happened to you?
- Can you even look back and, with the benefit of a bit of distance, see what Christ may have been doing that you have actually benefited from?

Prayer

Lord, this is a tough thing to take on board. I don't want you to feel distant! Help me, when you do, to go on trusting you. Help me take that sense of distance and be energized by it to seek you again. Amen.

11

Christ finds us beautiful

Love songs typically consist of lovers telling each other how beautiful they find each other and how much they desire each other: 'You are beautiful.' 'You are the one that I want!' This is also true of the spiritual romance – the mystical marriage of Christ and believers.

Early in the Song of Songs the two lovers coo to each other:

Man: Ah, you are beautiful, my love; ah, you are beautiful;
            your eyes are doves.
Woman: Ah, you are beautiful, my beloved, truly lovely.[1]

Later in their relationship it feels as though the passion has been turned up to full volume. The man announces his delight in the woman's beauty with a stream of extraordinary images:

How beautiful you are, my darling!
   Oh, how beautiful!
   Your eyes behind your veil are doves.
Your hair is like a flock of goats
   descending from the hills of Gilead.
Your teeth are like a flock of sheep just shorn,
   coming up from the washing.
Each has its twin;
   not one of them is alone.
Your lips are like a scarlet ribbon;
   your mouth is lovely.
Your temples behind your veil
   are like the halves of a pomegranate.

Your neck is like the tower of David,
    built with courses of stone;
on it hang a thousand shields,
    all of them shields of warriors.
Your breasts are like two fawns,
    like twin fawns of a gazelle
        that browse among the lilies.
Until the day breaks
    and the shadows flee,
I will go to the mountain of myrrh
    and to the hill of incense.
You are altogether beautiful, my darling;
    there is no flaw in you.
(Song 4:1–7)

Strange imagery!

What a strange rush of comparisons! 'Lips . . . like a scarlet ribbon' may cross the centuries easily enough, but most of the other similes would not go down particularly well on a Valentine's Day card. Perhaps we can just imagine that a flock of goats gracefully descending a hillside with long silky hair waving in the breeze is actually quite a flattering simile. But some of these comparisons seem to have had a special meaning in a different culture, which we have lost. The temple–pomegranate one feels like that to me. It may be that the actual physical resemblance is less important than we tend to think, and that what matters more is the symbolic meaning; for example, the sense of strength and majesty in the tower of David is like the majestic appearance of her neck. But it is a bit of a stretch for most of us to think that way: 'Your neck is like the London Shard' isn't going to go down well with most women. To say 'Your physical beauty matches your inner strength' might do rather better.

However, the main point is that seeing the woman gives the man an intense experience of pleasure. Interpreting this, as we let Jesus speak to us as the Lover of our soul, we must hear him expressing his pleasure in us and how he finds us beautiful.

Beautiful clothes

Earlier we encountered this idea, and saw how Christ's beauty covers and replaces our moral ugliness through his death on the cross so that now he finds us beautiful, clothed as we are with the robes of his righteousness. This is the primary picture, one we find reflected in a powerful moment in Revelation 7:

> After this I looked, and there before me was a great multitude that no one could count, from every nation, tribe, people and language, standing before the throne and before the Lamb. They were wearing white robes and were holding palm branches in their hands . . .
>
> These are they who have come out of the great tribulation; they have washed their robes and made them white in the blood of the Lamb.
> (Revelation 7:9, 14)

The white robes are a powerful picture of our justification, our being put right with God. And how that sight of white robes pleases Christ!

However, there is a little more to explore here, because in Revelation 19 we find another dimension to the 'white robe' theme:

> I heard what sounded like a great multitude, like the roar of rushing waters and like loud peals of thunder, shouting:
>
> 'Hallelujah!
>   For our Lord God Almighty reigns.
> Let us rejoice and be glad
>   and give him glory!
> For the wedding of the Lamb has come,
>   and his bride has made herself ready.
> Fine linen, bright and clean,
>   was given her to wear.'
> (Revelation 19:6–8a)

We expect to hear again that this is the 'alien righteousness' of Christ, the transfer of his beauty to us. But we are in for a surprise. John gives us an explanation of the beautiful clothes: 'Fine linen stands for the righteous acts of God's holy people' (Revelation 19:8b).

Their own lives are seen as fine linen. But how?

Growing beauty

As we grow as believers in Christ, we find his beauty grows in us. And that beauty pleases him! When I try to explain this to people, I often find a lot of scepticism. So, I point to what the Bible says about the ways in which believers can please God in this life, imperfect though we are:

- 'May these words of my mouth and this meditation of my heart be *pleasing* in your sight, LORD' (Psalm 19:14);
- 'May my meditation be *pleasing* to him, as I rejoice in the LORD' (Psalm 104:34);
- 'I urge you, brothers and sisters . . . to offer your bodies as a living sacrifice, holy and *pleasing* to God' (Romans 12:1);
- 'We make it our goal to *please* him, whether we are at home in the body or away from it' (2 Corinthians 5:9);
- 'We continually ask God to fill you with the knowledge of his will . . . so that you may live a life worthy of the Lord and *please* him in every way' (Colossians 1:9–10).[2]

Still unconvinced?

Do you have any lingering doubts that it is possible for believers to please God? You may find it hard to believe, but that list of examples shows us *beyond all argument* that pleasing him is something we can and should aim at.

What 'pleases'? Something that is good, true and beautiful. For God, goodness, truth and beauty are different ways of describing the same reality which he is pleased by. In the metaphor of the marriage relationship, which we are exploring in the Song of Songs, this means that Christ can be pleased by all sorts of things in us that he finds beautiful. This is what is promised in Isaiah 61:3, that Jesus will 'bestow on them a crown of beauty instead of ashes'.

Isaiah seems to have loved this idea. In the following references, the word translated 'splendour' could also be translated as 'glory' or 'beauty':

Isaiah 46:13   I will grant salvation to Zion,
                 my splendour to Israel.

Isaiah 49:3   He said to me, 'You are my servant,
                 Israel, in whom I will display my splendour.'

Isaiah 52:1   Awake, awake, Zion,
                 clothe yourself with strength!
                 Put on your garments of splendour,
                 Jerusalem, the holy city.

Isaiah 55:5   The LORD your God,
                 the Holy One of Israel . . .
                 has endowed you with splendour.

Isaiah 60:21 All your people . . .
                 are the shoot I have planted,
                 the work of my hands,
                 for the display of my splendour.

Isaiah 61:3   Those who grieve in Zion . . .
                 will be called oaks of righteousness,
                 a planting of the LORD
                 for the display of his splendour.[3]

A concise summary: Christ gives us his splendour; we put on Christ's splendour; we display Christ's splendour. Christ gives us his beauty; we put on Christ's beauty; we display Christ's beauty.

It's about you!

Yet I find Christians reluctant to receive these words for themselves. I remember staying with two people whom I admire for the sacrifices they have made for Christ and their commitment to the gospel. I was studying Isaiah. As I read the book, I felt that the words in Isaiah 55:5 – 'he has endowed you with splendour [= glory = beauty]' – were particularly true of them and so I shared that with them.

'I don't feel especially endowed with splendour' was the response. Perhaps that was part of the splendour – the humility that saw others as better than them. But it was also true that for an objective third-party observer like me, there was a beauty about their lives that Christ had given.

It is, of course, *his* beauty. 'The light of the Sun of Righteousness don't [*sic*] only shine upon them,' says Edwards of Christians, 'but is so communicated to them that they shine also, and become little images of that Sun which shines upon them.'[4]

The apostle Peter writes about how beautiful Christian women can be:

> Your beauty should not come from outward adornment, such as elaborate hairstyles and the wearing of gold jewellery or fine clothes. Rather, it should be that of your inner self, the unfading beauty of a gentle and quiet spirit, which is of great worth in God's sight.
> (1 Peter 3:3–4)

A 'gentle and quiet spirit' is beautiful. God sees it. He values such beauty highly and enormously. Outward beauty is comparatively superficial and short-lived. But there is an inner beauty that lasts for ever, which God loves. *And what is true for women is just as true for men!* Christ finds both believing women and men beautiful when he finds gentleness and quietness like his own. And he finds that beautiful. A writer from an earlier century puts it like this:

> Those who are Christ's are very lovely creatures and [must] have in themselves exceeding great loveliness, because there is to be found within them a work of his grace, a new creation, and a life that in some way adorns the gospel. The expressions used here give us ground to believe that Christ hath a great esteem of believers, however worthless they may be in themselves.[5]

Jesus anticipates our flustered objections: 'No, I'm not beautiful!' 'How can I be?' 'Look at me – how can you say that?' And he meets them with a powerful rebuttal: believers are never more beautiful in Christ's eyes than when their own spots are most obvious to themselves.

He finds it beautiful when we see our sin, admit our sin, make no attempt to conceal or minimize our sin, but lament our sin.

He does this by seeing what he is doing in us and enjoying the beauty he finds. As Matthew Henry says:

He takes great delight in the good work which his grace has wrought in the souls of believers, so that though they have their weaknesses, whatever they think of themselves, and the world thinks of them, he thinks them fair.[6]

It's a garden

I have a friend, a former colleague, who sees his inner life as a garden, with Christ as the gardener. Think of your inner life like that for a moment. A real garden is always a bit of a mixture. There are plants growing there in just the way the gardener wants. Other plants are a bit slow to grow, or to flower or produce fruit. Then there are the weeds which need constant attention.

Over time, really good gardeners are able, through the combination of time, effort, skill and persistence, to see a garden improve significantly. But on the way to achieving their goal, they will find things that please them – perhaps a cluster of lupins that push their delicate flowers heavenwards at just the right time, or a rosebush that does have some bindweed on the stem but also has a shower of gold-coloured blossoms.

Christ sees the bindweed and the sluggish fruit trees that are taking years to crop well. But he also sees the golden roses. And he finds them beautiful.

Spurgeon imagines Jesus explaining this to those who believe in him: 'I see Myself in your eyes; I can see My own beauty in you. And whatever belongs to Me, belongs to you.'[7]

Surely, this is how it is possible. Christ creates beauty in us, a beauty that is his and that he must naturally find beautiful. I have found that older writers, from earlier centuries, whom many regard as stern and fierce, are simultaneously the most gushing *and* the most careful to reason everything out theologically. What you do not find is the kind of simplistic 'God finds me beautiful unconditionally, just as I am' kind of statement that is common today. They know that that is misleading. But they also know that Jesus does find beauty in us.

Failure, regret and beauty

This truth even applies to our sense of failure! Here is Spurgeon again:

> You seem to have got just enough faith to know how unbelieving you are. You have got love, but somehow you have only got love enough to let you know how little you love Him! You have some humility, but you have only enough humility to discover you are very proud – you have some zeal for Christ, but you have only zeal enough to make you chide yourself that you are so cold! You have some hope, but you have only hope enough to lead you to see how despairing and desponding you often are; you have some patience, but you have only patience enough to teach you how often you murmur when you ought not. 'I confess,' you say, 'that all my graces are a stench in my own nostrils and all the good things I trust I have, I cannot look upon them with any pride or self-congratulation; I must bury myself in dust and ashes! And even those things, I can but weep over them, for they are so marred by my own evil nature.' But now then, the very things that you and I very properly weep over, Christ delights in! He loves all these. The smell may seem to be but very faint and feeble, yet Jesus observes it. Jesus smells it, Jesus loves it and Jesus approves it.[8]

Can you see the psychologically subtle, theologically careful way in which Spurgeon describes what Christ finds beautiful? Ironically, it is our regret at our *lack* of self-created beauty that so delights him. That humility is beautiful to him. He wins both ways! If there is some real growth in grace which even the most modest of us really cannot deny – 'I suppose it is true I don't swear any more' – that is beautiful to him. If we lament our failure out of genuine regret, *that* is beautiful to him too!

You come to church and, gosh, it's been a bad morning. You've got up late. It's been hard getting out of bed. If you have children, they've all argued. When you arrive at the building, you realize you've got odd socks on, you haven't brushed your hair, and you are in no kind of shape for worship.

The first hymn is done already. You find your seat – not the usual one because that's been taken by someone more punctual than you. That is oddly disconcerting. The service is proceeding and you're hardly following, but everyone else is standing so you do too and try to join in the next song. There is only one line that you feel you sing with any kind of real sincerity. The rest of it washes straight over you like someone trying to wash grease off a plate with no detergent. You're distracted and you're thinking: this is absolute rubbish. I'm getting nothing out of this at all. And I bet God hates it too.

But Jesus Christ loves the drops of honey falling off your tongue as you're worshipping him as much as you can.

Dane Ortlund uses a very similar illustration:

You have just been taken up into the Trinity. You have been swept up into the communal love and adoration that stretches back into time immemorial and the overflow of which caused the very universe to be brought into existence – so that you, on a bland Sunday morning, as a sinner, could participate in the joy of the triune God, Father delighting in Son, Son adoring Father, with the Holy Spirit being himself the very bond of love into which you are swept up. And though you will not take on new physical features when you leave church that morning, you will have been beautified, and the perceptive onlooker will note the difference in your countenance – a change which is a glimpse of the final state of paradise in the new heavens and the new earth.[9]

That really is you on that tricky Sunday morning! Christ sees the beauty in you, and delights in it.

Questions

- What is your reaction to the thought that Jesus finds you beautiful?
- What are the dangers in receiving this thought?
- What are the dangers in *not* receiving this thought?

Take a moment to think about the way you care about your physical appearance and feel either proud or sad about it. Compare that with the inner beauty which Christ is giving you, and which he loves.

Prayer

Lord, this is the most unbelievable truth. I find it hard to see myself as in any way beautiful – or, if I do, I start to get proud, which destroys the beauty! Please help me to know that you rejoice in the beauty you have given me. Help me to receive more of it! Amen.

12

Christ gets crazy with love

Jumping on to trains, crossing continents and oceans, getting up at unearthly hours for video calls, spending money we can't really spare on flowers and rings ... When we love someone, we do and say things that would be unimaginable otherwise.

God wants us to be crazy in our love for Christ, but what comes first is his love for us. In the last chapter we thought about Christ's delight in our beauty. Now we take things a step further as we think about his desire for us. There is a difference – the difference between looking at a photo and admiring someone's appearance, and talking to the person, lying entwined in his or her arms.

An unstoppable urge

In the first seven verses of Song chapter 4 the man speaks in raptures about the beauty of the woman he loves. For the rest of the chapter he describes the powerful desire this unleashes in him, a desire to become one flesh with her. He urges her to join him, so that she is no longer at a distance:

> Come with me from Lebanon, my bride,
>   come with me from Lebanon.
> Descend from the crest of Amana,
>   from the top of Senir, the summit of Hermon ...
> (Song 4:8)

They're looking up at Mount Hermon. It's a remote place and it's magnificent. It's awe-inspiring, but it's distant. We hear his insistence:

'Come with me, come with me.' He longs for her to move towards him, and him towards her.

What is driving this? He confesses ecstatically what has happened to him:

You have stolen my heart, my sister, my bride;
 you have stolen my heart
with one glance of your eyes,
 with one jewel of your necklace.
(Song 4:9)

This is the craziness of love.[1] It is more than appreciation: it is passion, overriding everything, a magnificent obsession, a driving force unlike any other, stronger even than hatred. The eighteenth-century poet Alexander Pope describes this same experience of one physical aspect of a woman capturing a man:

Fair tresses man's imperial race ensnare,
and beauty draws us with a single hair.[2]

Divine passion

The lover of the Song feels the power of love and cannot resist it. Understanding these words as the words of Christ the Lover of our souls to us, we must hear the passion they express. Of course, divine passion is different from human passion: this is in the Bible to make us feel *wanted*. This expression of love tells us that Christ's heart is locked on to us immovably in love and desire. I know that seems as though it must be an exaggeration, but given that the Song is about his love for me, these must be his words to me, and I cannot brush them aside in disbelief or embarrassment.

The young man moves on further from appreciation to desire. The imagery switches now: 'You are a garden locked up' (Song 4:12a) – or, as the New Living Translation puts it, 'You are my private garden.'

A lovely garden

This kind of garden is a common feature of Ancient (and modern) Near Eastern life – the walled garden, with good water supplies ('you are a spring enclosed, a sealed fountain', Song 4:12b), which is tenderly and skilfully cultivated to produce a kind of mini-paradise. It's a potent image. The garden is enclosed and locked. You need a key to go in. It is a truly stunning image for both human sexuality and human spirituality, somewhere special and private. Listen to how exotically it is planted:

> Your plants are an orchard of pomegranates
> > with choice fruits,
> > with henna and nard,
> > nard and saffron,
> > calamus and cinnamon,
> > with every kind of incense tree,
> > with myrrh and aloes
> > and all the finest spices.
> (Song 4:13–14)

This combination of plants would have been botanically impossible, literally impossible, unless there were heated greenhouses and controlled microclimates all over the garden. The plants described here come from two or three continents which experience different climates. So, to have them all in one single garden just wouldn't have worked.

A magic garden

Here we find a highly idealized picture of a magic garden in which the most luscious fruits from all over the known world are combined. Notice the emphasis on the sense of smell: the fragrances, the sweet incense. It creates a sensory overload – who could possibly smell and taste all these things at once? In the ancient world some of these gardens that were locked away were particularly beautiful and special, and reserved for kings and royalty and wealthy people. They were places where pleasure just ran riot. That is how the woman's sexuality is described.

The garden is well watered, a metaphor standing for the way God himself nurtures our capacity for intimacy, human and divine:

You are a garden fountain,
a well of flowing water
streaming down from Lebanon.
(Song 4:15)

A garden with a meaning

This is a picture of the Bible's vision for human sexual flourishing, showing that our sexuality is something that needs protection, and to be kept private and reserved, because it is a pleasure garden of the highest order. It is locked away for the right time, but at the right time it becomes just a wonderful place of pleasure and joy and even sensory overload. The Bible is very balanced here. It's not repressive about sexuality, but it says that these things need to be locked away and kept for the right moment to be enjoyed.

As we apply this to human relationships, we see the positive centre of the Bible's insistence on sexual love being reserved for marriage. It provides a part of what has been called 'a better story'[3] and 'a better vision'[4] for human flourishing than the no-holds-barred approach of modern Western society.

Your inner garden

As we apply this to our relationship with Christ, we are on delicate ground, but it is right to try to live in the metaphor as long as our imaginations are shaped by the gospel! Every human being has a garden in his or her soul. It is intended to be rich, fragrant, enticing and beautiful, arousing Christ's desire to sit in it and enjoy its fruits. But sin spoils that place. We fail to tend the garden to make it attractive to Christ; we let the wrong things enter it, thinking we can have mutual pleasure with them there. But those expectations are never matched with the reality.

This applies particularly to our sexuality and our relationships. So often, people look to them for the kind of intimacy which only Christ offers, and are left feeling disappointed and resentful. It can apply to all kinds of other things too – homes, possessions, careers, special kinds of sensory pleasure, such as concerts or gourmet food or unusual experiences like exotic travel, hang gliding and extreme sports. We sense that we have that special locked garden and try to enjoy it.

But that place is only suited to Christ. In the gospel he recreates it – as prophesied:

> They will be like a well-watered garden,
>   and they will sorrow no more.
> (Jeremiah 31:12)

Jesus longs to dwell in it and enjoy it. He desires us! No garden is too trampled on, polluted, overgrown with weeds or damaged for the Master Gardener, the Holy Spirit, to make a place for Christ to enjoy. Not even mine, and not even yours. He desires that place within you. I am tempted to say that he salivates at the thought of intimacy there.

Inviting him in

The woman responds to the man's vision of her beautiful virginity by saying:

> Awake, north wind,
>   and come, south wind!
> Blow on my garden,
>   that its fragrance may spread everywhere.
> Let my beloved come into his garden
>   and taste its choice fruits.
> (Song 4:16)

She wants the fragrance which he loves so much to spread. She wants him to come in. She wants him to eat. It's one man in the sealed garden at the right time, not all manner of men at different times. One writer suggests: 'Untainted virginity is the best wedding gift one can give to a spouse.'[5] Whether it's the best gift is a good question,[6] but certainly it is a very great gift. We will return to that in a later chapter, as more needs to be said not least for those who have lost their virginity outside marriage and wish they could recreate it. For now, though, let us note that she yields willingly to his desire – and ask ourselves: will we yield to Christ's desire for intimacy with us?

Back to verse 9:

You have stolen my heart, my sister, my bride;
    you have stolen my heart
with one glance of your eyes,
    with one jewel of your necklace.

We remember his appreciation of her hair as silky goat hair (4:1).

Getting personal

After having surgery on my spine a while ago, I had to spend hours and hours on my back, sedated but still in pain. I distracted myself with DVD box sets and dropped into wondering why the surgeon's prediction of a much quicker recovery had been so wrong. I found I could pray for other people a bit more than usual with the extra time. But often I just lay there quietly.

Again and again, I felt Christ moving closer. Sometimes I had to make the first move; sometimes he did. This image from the poem kept coming to mind: his delight in the light on a single hair on his beloved's head.

These are biblical pictures of the delight of Jesus Christ in us, each one of us who has faith in him. They are given to us to help us understand and to feel his love, not in theory but in practice, the sweet reality of the invisible God drawing near, for example to a (temporarily) disabled middle-aged man lying on his back in pain – and to you too.

Spurgeon imagines Christ explaining this to an unconvinced Christian:

> You have praised Me, I will praise you; you think much of Me, I think quite as much of you. You use great expressions for Me, I will use just the same for you. You say My love is better than wine, so is yours to Me. You tell Me all My garments smell of myrrh, so do yours. You say My word is sweeter than honey to your lips, so is yours to Mine; all that you can say of Me, I say it to you. I see Myself in your eyes, I can see My own beauty in you. And whatever belongs to Me, belongs to you. Therefore, O My love, I will sing back the song – you have sung it to your beloved and I will sing it to My beloved. You have sung it to your husband, I will sing it to My sister, My spouse.[7]

Listen to the words of your divine Lover in the Song, feel his desire, realize it is for you – and yield to him.

Questions

- How does the idea of Christ being 'crazy with love' for you strike you?
- What does he want in return from you?

Prayer

Oh Lord, do you really desire me? Really? How can you? Why? But it says in your Word that you do. Help me to feel your love. I want you in return. Help me to yield myself willingly to you. Amen.

13
Finally, the wedding!

How on earth did we manage before we had spreadsheets? Modern weddings would never happen without them. Such tools never reach capacity. You can add the hundreds of rows that are needed – for the micro-timing of the day, for the different kinds of pre-dinner snacks (vegan, vegetarian, carnivore, coeliac, non-dairy), for the personalized little bottles of gin for each guest,[1] for the three dozen photo groups, for the battle order in which the bride, her father, the bridesmaids and page boys will glide down the aisle, like a naval formation steaming into battle in the grand old days of the British Navy.

As well as these practical details, it is likely that the bride and groom are experiencing all sorts of feelings, including anticipating their first night together. That will not appear in the spreadsheet, but it is at least as important as anything in it.

Moving towards consummation

Writers have found it hard to agree on a precise dramatic sequence for the relationship at the heart of the Song of Songs, but in chapters 1 – 4 there is a general sense of progression towards marriage. One clue is the vision in Song 3:6–10 of Solomon's carriage arriving from the wilderness for his wedding day. Some feel that this is literally Solomon's wedding and they construct a story to accommodate it. Others feel that it is like a modern British bride saying, 'It's my wedding day and I am going to be a princess.' David and Victoria Beckham were rather mocked for sitting on purple and gold thrones at their wedding, but they were only acting out physically how many brides and grooms expect to feel – like royalty. That is how I take it.

The implication is that a wedding is anticipated and is seen in royal terms.

In chapter 4 the man bursts out in raptured appreciation of the beauty of his beloved. As the chapter progresses, rapture becomes more and more physical as he anticipates lovemaking. It is as though we track the inner life of a bridegroom as the wedding gets closer and closer. We hear the woman give her consent in Song 4:16.

A tasteful veil

Then there is a gap in the action! The Song of Songs is undeniably an erotic poem, but it is the most tasteful and discreet kind of eroticism. So, unlike almost all other writing about sex which virtually always in the end tips over the edge into unhelpful explicitness, the Song pulls down a discreet curtain through its use of metaphors – which express desire and pleasure but do so in ways that are not linked explicitly to physical details.

The description of the couple's wedding night ends with her saying 'Ready for you'. The night passes, and the next we hear is the husband looking back on it – discreetly but appreciatively:

I have come into my garden, my sister, my bride;
    I have gathered my myrrh with my spice.
I have eaten my honeycomb and my honey;
    I have drunk my wine and my milk.
(Song 5:1)

He uses the metaphors of smell and taste to express how delightful their first night together was. That is as much as we need! The imagery shows just that it's been intensely pleasurable for him, but he doesn't go into graphic physical detail. The text simply says that this has been a wonderful, beautiful consummation of their relationship.

How can we apply this?

Before we reach to the spiritual meaning, however, I need to interject a gentle pastoral warning. This is a highly idealized account of a wedding night. This is how a wedding night would be in paradise.

In practice, all sorts of factors mean that the heights of sexual pleasure often require trial and error.[2] But that is not our main concern here.

Christ's wedding night?

How does this relate to our experience of Christ? We need to realize that this is primarily about *his* experience of us! It seems to me valid to see it in three stages.

1 Conversion

First of all, this relates to the intimacy that Christ has with us when we yield to him in the surrender of conversion and allow him to take over our lives. Our inner gardens are not yet what they will be, but we are ready to let his Holy Spirit start renovating them. He anticipates the joy that will come; even our simple brokenness and receptivity is sweet-smelling to him. This is the rejoicing in heaven at one sinner repenting, one lost sheep being found.

2 Recurring joy

The English theologian John Owen loved Christ, and loved to write about the love of Christ. He knew that Christ took pleasure in him, and this is how he describes it:

> Thoughts of communion with the saints were the joy of his heart from eternity . . . his soul rejoiced in the thoughts of that pleasure and delight which he would take in them. Christ delights exceedingly in his saints. [A person's wedding day] is the most unmixed delight that [many people experience]. The delight of the bridegroom in the day of his marriage is the height of what an expression of delight can [rise to]. Christ has this response in himself because of the relationship he takes us into. His heart is glad in us.

Then Owen thought he would really drive it home. We might have been thinking that it all lies in the future, when we are presented to Jesus 'radiant . . . without stain or wrinkle or any other blemish' (Ephesians 5:27), and that right now we are far from radiant. There are stains aplenty; our spiritual faces are covered with disfiguring wrinkles and the kind of blemishes you need plastic surgery for. But Owen will have none of that. This is how he smashes our doubts and fears. At the top of his voice, he bellows across the centuries: 'And every day whilst we live is his wedding day.'[3]

I love that whole quotation, and use it as often as I think I can get away with it in talks and sermons. I often find my voice cracking with emotion as I read it out, but if I can manage it, when I get to the last sentence, I find myself shouting jubilantly, 'And every day whilst we live is his wedding day!'

3 Repeated experience

This is therefore a repeated experience. Christ draws near to us in desire, and we open ourselves to receive him. While this is not something that is under our control, it is something we can become aware of.

We bring to mind a biblical text about Christ's love, perhaps even this one from the Song of Songs (5:1). We think about him as the one who eats supper with sinners, who moves towards the unclean and, touching them, makes them whole.

We then attend to the movement of Christ towards, into, within us. We may become aware of a gentle pressure, of his knocking. Or it may be simply a sense of a real presence, as when we are feeling rather sad and lost but, hearing a small sound behind us, we find there is a friend sitting quietly in the same room smiling at us. In either case, we need to make ourselves receptive to Christ. The welcome the bride gives to her groom is a good model for us: 'Let my beloved come into his garden' (Song 4:16b).

Then we sit (or lie or walk), and attend to his presence, perhaps particularly noting that this is not all about us, for he has come in for his own pleasure more than ours. Most of the time it is not felt like a thunderstorm, but rather a few gentle spots of cool rain. We know by faith he is there. We receive him in love.

I am suggesting that, for Christ, Song 5:1 represents our initial opening to him, and then repeated patterns of our receiving him in the ordinary spiritual intimacy of the Christian life, lived by faith, not sight.

The final fulfilment

The verse also points to a deeper, fuller, perfect and complete experience of intimacy which we will know at the return of Christ. The marriage metaphor, which keeps popping up again in the Bible like rocky granite outcrops revealing what underlies the whole landscape, has a final culmination and consummation. Jesus compares the time between his death and his return to the time before a bridegroom rejoins his guests (Matthew 9:15). He warns people about being ready for his return, through parables about wedding attendants being ready for a bridegroom (Matthew 25:1–13) and guests being invited to a wedding banquet (Matthew 22:1–14).

In the book of Revelation John sees and hears that great day with the prophetic imagination of faith, reaching forward into what will be. He is granted a further vision of the same event in Revelation 21:2: 'I saw the Holy City, the new Jerusalem, coming down out of heaven from God, prepared as a bride beautifully dressed for her husband.'

This is the ultimate climactic intimacy. This is the moment to which all positive experiences of earthly pleasure and intimacy point. Equally, all our disappointments with intimacy point here too, because the text here tells us that finally we will be touched in the deepest place and in the most sensitive of ways. This is something that even the most happily married person or most contented single person has not experienced in this life.

The climax of history

That's what the whole of human history is pointing to. That's what marriage itself was created to point to. All human sexuality is a set of signposts to this, because there will be no marriage in the new creation; such things will be done away with. We will have stronger, better, more intense relationships, but they won't be marital and sexual. These are metaphors pointing to something greater that is coming when Christ joins with his people.

Message to the aching heart

That is a special comfort to those of us with disappointments and regrets, or a sense of missing out, in the area of relationships and sexuality and marriage.

Undeniably, many people have an aching space inside for something that could have been – maybe because they've been widowed; maybe because they've never been married. For some, marriage is difficult or disappointing in some way. There is a space, a sense of incompleteness in this life, pointing them towards the great fulfilment, the return of Christ.

I can assure you 100 per cent that when you meet Jesus in glory and you see his face looking into your eyes, you're not going to be saying to him, 'You gave me a really raw deal on earth because my marriage was unhappy.' You're just not going to be doing that then. You will not be complaining to him, 'Well, it *is* great being in heaven, but I wish I'd had more sex on earth. It was just unfair.' No one's going to be saying that.

It is impossible properly to imagine that moment, but it is worth trying, and letting others help us to imagine it. Peter Masters is particularly helpful here:

To see Him will have an impact upon us similar to seeing and sensing all the most spectacular and precious sights and experiences added together. We may think of the most wonderful feeling of relief and gratitude we have ever experienced, when perhaps some terrible fear was removed. We may add to this the deepest sensation of love we have ever felt, and also the most humbling sense of awe and wonder.

Then we may add the greatest surge of excitement we have ever encountered, along with the most powerful thrill of triumph that ever swept over us. Finally, we may combine with all these the most profound amazement at breathtaking scenes of beauty and power that we have ever experienced. If we take all these magnificent impressions together, the very best of earthly sensations, magnified many times, we will have some small sense of the majesty and wonder of seeing Christ Jesus our Lord.[4]

Perfect mutual delight

We should remember that this is mutual pleasure, like the mutual delight of a groom and a bride.

Here is another older writer who has thought hard about this. He expresses the results of his thinking in a prayer. It is written as continuous prose, but I have broken up the lines to encourage you to pause and absorb as much as you can of each one before moving on:

> Let us . . . come to see ourselves in Thy beauty in everlasting
>   life.
> That is:
> Let me be so transformed in Thy beauty,
> that, being alike in beauty,
> we may see ourselves both in Thy beauty;
> having Thy beauty,
> so that, one beholding the other,
> each may see his own beauty in the other,
> the beauty of both being Thine only,
> and mine absorbed in it.
>
> And thus I shall see Thee in Thy beauty,
> and myself in Thy beauty,
> and Thou shalt see me in Thy beauty;
> and I shall see myself in Thee in Thy beauty,
> and Thou Thyself in me in Thy beauty;
> so shall I seem to be Thyself in Thy beauty,
> and Thou myself in Thy beauty;

my beauty shall be Thine,
Thine shall be mine,
and I shall be Thou in it,
and Thou myself in Thine own beauty;
for Thy beauty will be my beauty,
and so we shall see, each the other, in Thy beauty.

This is the adoption of the sons of God,
who may truly say what the Son Himself [said] to the Eternal
    Father:
'All My things are Thine,
and Thine are Mine . . .'[5]

I imagine that you will have to read this more than once, and even then you may feel a bit stretched. It is a stunning vision of our union with Christ in his beauty. God wants us to see that vision in the great wedding party of Christ's return. Only then will we be able to take in fully what he feels fully now.

Song 5:1 not only tells us that we're going to enjoy the wedding party tremendously; it also points to Christ's pleasure on that day. I hesitate to say it, and I use this language in human terms because we cannot know what it is to live in eternity, but *he's* looking forward to it. *He's* anticipating that wedding day, the eating of the honeycomb, the drinking of the wine, the smelling of the perfume which he's already preparing in the garden of our souls.

When you have a telescope, you can look through the wrong end (which makes everything look much further away than it is). Or you can look through the right end, and the distance is compressed for a moment. Too many of us have the telescope of faith turned the wrong way round, and Christ looks further away. Too many of us are so fixated on this life, particularly on what's not going well for us, with life's disappointments. The telescope is turned the other way, and heaven just seems further away even than it does without it.

Song 5:1 makes us turn the telescope the right way round. Christ invites us to look at that day through the lens of this text and make it more real, more immediate. This text is intended to offer healing for our greyness and grumpiness. As we struggle in this life, we look through the telescope and we see the wedding feast, the perfect world and the glory that will be ours for all eternity. We see that we have not missed out on anything that matters because we are heading into the centre of the universe and of all history, to which marriage and sexuality point – and to which all singleness and unexpressed sexuality points too – the final climax of intimacy that will be ours in Christ.

Questions

- How much time do you spend thinking about the next life?
- How could the above help you to cope with what you do not have in this life, and to meditate on what you will have then, for ever?

Prayer

Lord, to know you is joy unimaginable. But it never seems to last. Thank you that one day it will be all joy. Amen.

14

Not tonight, dear!

A wife anonymously posted online a document which her husband had sent her, listing her reasons for not wanting to make love (see the spreadsheet).[1]

	A	B	C	D	E	F	G
1							
2	DATE	SEX?	EXCUSE				
3	2014-06-03	No	"I'm watching the show" (*Friends* re-run)				
4	2014-06-04	No	"I feel sweaty and gross, I need a shower" (didn't shower until next morning)				
5	2014-06-06	No	(non-verbal)				
6	2014-06-09	No	"I'm exhausted"				
7	2014-06-10	Yes					
8	2014-06-11	No	"I'm still a bit tender from yesterday"				
9	2014-06-12	No	(non-verbal)				
10	2014-06-13	No	"I'm trying to watch the movie" (fell asleep 15 min later)				
11	2014-06-16	No	"I'm too drunk and I ate too much"				
12	2014-06-18	No	"I won't have time to get showered and ready for dinner" (we were 20 min early)				
13	2014-06-19	No	"I just came back from the gym, I feel gross" (didn't shower until next morning)				
14	2014-06-20	No	(non-verbal)				
15	2014-06-21	No	"I have to be up early"				
16	2014-06-22	No	(non-verbal)				
17	2014-06-27	Yes					
18	2014-06-29	No	"You're too drunk"				
19	2014-06-30	No	"I feel gross"				
20	2014-07-01	No	"I'm not feeling good, I ate too much"				
21	2014-07-03	No	"I'm sweaty and gross, and I'm tired"				
22	2014-07-04	No	(non-verbal)				
23	2014-07-05	No	"I might be getting sick"				
24	2014-07-06	No	"I still don't feel 100%"				
25	2014-07-10	No	"I need a shower, I feel gross"				
26	2014-07-11	No	"I'm too tired"				
27	2014-07-12	Yes					
28	2014-07-13	No	"No"				
29	2014-07-14	No	(non-verbal)				
30	2014-07-16	No	"I'm watching my show, I don't want to miss anything"				
31							
32							

Interestingly, we find one line of a 'spreadsheet' like this in Song of Songs 5:3! But we have to start a couple of verses earlier:

I slept but my heart was awake.
    Listen! My beloved is knocking . . .
(Song 5:2a)

It seems likely that the man and woman are now married. The first verse of Song chapter 5 appears to show him looking back in raptured appreciation of their wedding night. But now they face an argument!

A nightmare

Some readers take this passage simply as a literal description, but many have pointed to all sorts of features that make it sound more like a kind of dream sequence. There are bits here that don't quite fit with what would have been the literal reality of a newly wedded couple. Would he really have been coming and knocking on her door in this way, and later, would she really have been going out in the streets at night, not properly dressed? It feels like a nightmare. We feel that there's a kind of disturbing quality about it, a vividness, with sudden cinematic movements from one part to another. At the start the woman even says, 'I slept but my heart was awake' (5:2a). That invites us to think about something that's going on inside her head in sleep. My own view is that we should read it as this kind of disjointed, alarming dream sequence, but also recognize that it speaks of an actual reality.

She hears him knocking on the door. (The door to her bedroom? We are not told.) His intentions are clear: lovemaking. He wants to come in, out of the wet night, to his beloved wife:

Open to me, my sister, my darling,
    my dove, my flawless one.
(Song 5:2b)

He wants to come to her. She offers what the poem presents as a flimsy excuse – 'I can't be bothered to get out of bed. Do I really have to?' – with the words:

I have taken off my robe –
  must I put it on again?
I have washed my feet –
  must I soil them again?
(Song 5:3)

You will probably say, 'Isn't that her choice? Isn't she allowed to do that?' That's a good question. There was a time when, within English law, husbands and wives were regarded as having what was called a conjugal right, a right to sex, more or less on demand, which was, as has been recently recognized, in effect a kind of licence for rape within marriage because the law said that marriage implied consent.

Although people tried to base the law on biblical principles, this isn't at all what God's Word says. The Bible insists on the principle of consent within sex, but it also says, notably in 1 Corinthians 7:1–7, that within marriage, husbands and wives will be making love to each other. Of course, there are times when one or the other will just not want to make love, and it is absolutely his or her right to say 'no'. However, biblically, for that to go on and on and on without good reason points to an issue that needs open discussion. Here, in the logic and narrative flow of the poem, the woman is offering flimsy reasons that don't hold together.

Saying 'no' to Jesus?

I am going to bypass any further application to married people so that we can think about this scene as it represents Christ our divine Lover drawing near and wanting to be close to us. He is knocking on the door of our souls.

This speaks of what happens to us when Jesus draws near to us in love, and then we say 'no' to opening the door. We say, 'Oh, I can't be bothered . . . I don't want to get out of bed. I don't want to get my feet dirty again.'

At the heart of our relationships with Christ lies this constant movement: he is coming and knocking on a steady, loving, inviting basis, saying, 'Will you let me in again so I can be intimate with you?'

Standing at the door

It is common for people to say that the Song of Songs is not quoted or referred to in the New Testament. But there is a probable echo of the Song in Jesus' letter to the church in Laodicea in Revelation 3:20: 'Here I am! I stand at the door and knock. If anyone hears my voice and opens the door, I will come in and eat with that person, and they with me.'

He comes, he knocks, he requests entry, he wants intimacy. That is what Christ does for our souls. The Song of Songs simply puts it in terms of a marriage metaphor rather than a guest metaphor. This is Christ's constant movement towards us.

How this happens varies from person to person and from time to time. Sometimes we suddenly become aware, in whatever way, of the presence of Christ. That may be a rare thing for some, perhaps more common for others. Maybe some of us could be more attuned to it. Suddenly, we've become aware of the reality of Christ, and that in that moment he is moving towards us. How will we respond in that moment?

Is he knocking?

More commonly, the approach of Christ is there in the normal routines of life. As we are deciding whether or not to read the Bible each day, Jesus is knocking at the door. That moment when you have to make a decision at 7 a.m. whether you get out of bed and wash your face and read your Bible for five or ten minutes or whether you stay in bed for another half an hour: that's the moment of the knocking, the Bridegroom at the door.

Or it may be that as you wake up, you have a choice: which will come first – Bible or phone?[2] Your Bridegroom is saying to you, 'Open for me, my darling, my dove, my flawless one', using words of endearment in that microsecond after waking when you are thinking that the most important thing right now is to check those emails. Jesus Christ is knocking on the door and saying, 'Let's have this quiet time together. Let's eat together. Let's start the day together.' Are you just going to say, 'I can't be bothered to get out of bed or listen to your voice rather than the voice of my social media page'?

In the Song, the man makes a further move which seems to trigger something in the woman:

My beloved thrust his hand through the latch-opening;
my heart began to pound for him.
(Song 5:4)

The return of desire

Maybe the further move reminds her that actually what she's saying is flimsy and inadequate, and that she does want him after all. The picture of her hands dripping with myrrh may be a poetic way of expressing her newly reawakened desire:

I arose to open for my beloved,
and my hands dripped with myrrh,
my fingers with flowing myrrh,
on the handles of the bolt.
(Song 5:5)

But by then it's too late. He's gone, and her heart sinks. She goes out and she looks for him, but she cannot find him. She calls, but there's no answer. She's lost him for this moment. Again, we should think of this not so much in the physical location of the city as in the emotional setting. This is what can open up within any relationship, as we saw earlier: distance. The woman says:

I opened for my beloved,
but my beloved had left; he was gone.
My heart sank at his departure.
(Song 5:6a)

Here we see what can happen dynamically when Christ draws near to us but we are too busy or preoccupied or cosy to respond. As before, this provides a biblical way of understanding his 'withdrawals' and working through them. The incident is similar to the one at the start of Song chapter 3, but there is a crucial difference. Then we did not know why he was absent. Here it is because she rebuffed him, then changed her mind, and he has withdrawn. She is determined to find him and goes out to look, but he is not to be found:

> I looked for him but did not find him.
> I called him but he did not answer.
> (Song 5:6b)

It's a picture of real-world relationships in which our intimacy varies at different times, and it goes up and down. The same is true of our experience of our love relationship with Christ.

Seeking and not finding

The woman's search then takes a terrifying turn:

> The watchmen found me
> as they made their rounds in the city.
> They beat me, they bruised me;
> they took away my cloak,
> those watchmen of the walls!
> (Song 5:7)

To be honest, I'm not quite sure how to interpret that. If we read it entirely literally, it is hard to think of any legitimate reason for the men to attack and strip her. It feels like a nightmare. In a nightmare something absolutely horrible happens that would not happen in real life, but it expresses our sense of pain or loss. It may be that the attack represents the woman's own feeling of woundedness, of the loss of the relationship. That feels like life beating you up.

A hidden Lord but a deeper work

One effect of the times when Jesus seems to withdraw is to make us long for him all the more, and to seek him and that conscious sense of his peace and presence. If you're in a state where God seems distant, seems inaccessible, please realize that this does not mean he is not working in you. He is there, but his Spirit is doing a different work when you don't feel his presence but instead feel a sense of absence. That sense of absence is given to you by God to make you seek after him all the more because you feel so incomplete without him.

The young woman comes to her female friends – the 'daughters of Jerusalem' – and says, 'Tell him I am faint with love' (5:8). She means she is in a distressing place. A sense of absence is designed to make you realize how unfulfilled you are by anything else. God himself will give you that sense of unfulfilled desire, of emptiness within, to make you charge off to him all the more earnestly. You're not aware of it being him, but it *is* him, and it's to propel you towards him all the more.

Before we see how the daughters of Jerusalem replied, we need to stop and linger with the woman in this state of distance and loss. William Cowper, whom we met earlier and whose mental illness deeply affected his sense of the love of Christ, wrote a poem which draws on this part of the Song:

To those who love the Lord I speak;
Is my Beloved near?
The Bridegroom of my soul I seek,
Oh! when will He appear?

Though once a man of grief and shame,
Yet now He fills a throne,
And bears the greatest, sweetest name,
That earth or heaven have known.

Grace flies before, and love attends
His steps where e'er He goes;
Though none can see Him but His friends,
And they were once His foes.

He speaks – obedient to His call
Our warm affections move:

Did He but shine alike on all,
Then all alike would love.

Then love in every heart would reign,
And war would cease to roar;
And cruel and bloodthirsty men
Would thirst for blood no more.

Such Jesus is, and such His grace;
Oh, may He shine on you!
And tell Him, when you see His face,
I long to see Him, too.[3]

This is poignant beyond words. Cowper echoes the woman in the Song in asking for help from friends. If that is you today, realize today you are not alone.

It may not be you, and if so, perhaps you need to linger on the picture of Christ knocking on the door of your soul wanting fresh intimacy on a *daily* basis.

A new mother was particularly touched by this thought:

The picture of Jesus knocking on the door when we might feel tempted not to bother with a quiet time was so helpful to me this morning, with [my husband] away and [my baby] to look after. Such a positive way of reframing the internal battle. Meeting with him this morning was a precious reward.

Christ invites you to do the same.

But you may need also to think about the ways in which you have been pushing him away. It could be many things.

In the next two chapters we are going to think about how sexual sin and pornography in particular are effectively our way of saying to Christ, 'Keep your distance; I have a better lover.'

Questions

- How do you identify with this particular 'nightmare' picture?
- If it doesn't feel much like your own experience, does it help you to understand someone else's loss of the felt presence of Christ?

Prayer

Lord, I know at times that you draw near and I draw back. Please forgive me. Please help me to sense you approaching me in your Word. Help me to receive you more consistently. Amen.

15

Spiritual intimacy betrayed and lost through porn

Meet the Jones Family:

Steve
Steve is a 49-year-old Christian. For the past twenty years he has struggled with pornography. Nobody knows, and he is full of self-hatred, shame and guilt. He is desperate to conquer this problem, but has little hope of change, and is concerned about how the problem seems to be getting worse.

Sarah
Sarah is Steve's wife. They have been married for twenty years. She is concerned about her ten-year-old son's internet and tablet use, and often finds new technology a little overwhelming. She was distraught when he downloaded a gaming app on the iPad and 'out of nowhere' explicit images appeared on the screen. Sarah suspects Steve looks at pornography, but the idea upsets her and makes her feel betrayed and insecure, so she tends to ignore her questions.

Susie
Susie is Steve and Sarah's eldest daughter. She is sixteen and regularly views porn. As a Christian she wishes this could stop, but doesn't know what to do, or who to talk to. Susie's friends at school think porn is normal and harmless, and often laugh about it. They regularly send her links to porn videos and websites in their group text.[1]

That is a fictional family. But there are many real Christian families who look rather similar.

Pornography in words and pictures is millennia old. But the development of the internet and of smartphones and other portable devices has made it much more easily accessible than previous generations could have imagined. The effects are deeply harmful and widespread.

Forfeiting real intimacy

It may seem strange to include these two 'extra' chapters in a book of this nature, but I believe they are absolutely essential. In today's world porn is one of the biggest ways in which Christians are spoiling and forfeiting their intimacy with Christ. As a pastor, I am aware that in private this affects many, many Christians. So, in a book about growing in spiritual intimacy, it is vital to look at one of the major blockages.

What we are talking about is looking at, reading, hearing and even interacting with sexually stimulating material, often though not always online, and/or accompanied by habits of frequent masturbation.[2]

What is happening here? A number of things, and there could be many starting points too. The theme of this book – finding pathways of spiritual intimacy with Jesus, the Lover of our souls – pushes us towards understanding the sins associated with porn and masturbation within that framework – and finding forgiveness and release within that framework too!

Not before time

Repeatedly in the Song of Songs we hear a warning about what the 1980s two-tone band, The Specials, called 'Too Much Too Young'.[3] The young woman in the Song puts it this way:

Daughters of Jerusalem, I charge you
    by the gazelles and by the does of the field:

do not arouse or awaken love
  until it so desires.
(Song 2:7; see also 3:5; 8:4)

These are important moments in the Song, all the more so for being repeated. The Song celebrates human desire, male and female beauty, romantic passion, erotic feelings, sexual attraction and physical sexual love. There is a deep awareness that these are like a caged tiger. Release them in the wrong way or at the wrong time and they will eat you alive! At different points it can feel as though the woman is talking to herself, as well as to her friends: 'Be careful! Don't get ahead of yourself! Watch out! Make sure you are not going beyond what is right.'

Managing our feelings

Managing sexual desire and attraction is part of growing up, from the very first hormonal stirrings of adolescence. As we become aware of our sexual capacity and instincts, we need to learn to control them and to avoid their premature expression.

The Song of Songs portrays sexual intimacy and romantic intimacy as good things, needing careful hedges around them. By contrast, porn use and uncontrolled masturbation are simply bad for you. The problem, though, is that it doesn't *feel* that way. When I have asked guys struggling with porn why they keep turning to it, again and again the answer is that it delivers intense pleasure, albeit of a rather short-lived nature. Then it leaves them feeling guilty, defeated and isolated. Two experts in the field, Wendy and Larry Maltz, sum it up: 'Porn is an extremely alluring and compelling product, capable of delivering sexual pleasure while at the same time setting one up for great pain.'[4]

Porn's effects

These experts go on to list nine of the most common serious negative consequences of using porn:

- 'I'm easily irritated and depressed';
- 'I've become isolated from other people';
- 'I'm sexually objectifying people';
- 'I'm neglecting important areas of my life';
- 'I'm making my partner unhappy';
- 'I'm feeling bad about myself';
- 'I'm having problems with sex';
- 'I'm engaging in risky and dangerous behaviour';
- 'I've become addicted to porn'.[5]

Real lives

Here are some real-life examples:

I was a slave to my addiction. I was such a slave that I didn't even understand that freedom existed.[6]

Porn has created a huge gap between the kind of woman I want to be with and the kind of woman I actually desire sexually.[7]

Porn doesn't have any long-term benefits, just long-term costs. My life is much better now without porn. I could have saved myself and other people a lot of grief if I'd never got involved with it in the first place.[8]

Sean was a church youth-group leader with a compulsive porn habit. He admitted:

I recognized the contradiction between what I said I believe and what porn was putting into my head. Even though I wasn't physically committing adultery . . . I was doing it in my mind. I realized my spiritual beliefs and my porn use cannot coexist peacefully in my life. I can't lead a youth group where I have a meaningful spiritual experience, [then] go home and [look at porn]. It isn't congruent.[9]

Here is the story of Bethany, also a Christian:

> [She] first came across online pornography at the age of eleven. [Now a woman in her twenties,] she describes how she could access 'risqué' material on YouTube, despite parental control filters. She told the *Daily Mail* how the easy-to-access porn warped her own relationships with boys. 'I did not want a relationship and assumed that no one would want me anyway, because of my pornography habit,' she said. 'It made me self-conscious about my looks – I didn't look like the girls on screen.'
>
> During her time at university her addiction grew to the point at which she left a lecture to get her fix. Speaking of the resulting guilt and shame she felt, she explained, 'I assumed I would be single for the rest of my life. I used porn to fill my loneliness.' Bethany finally opened up to a counsellor at her local church eighteen months ago and was 'gobsmacked' to learn of other women struggling with the same addiction. She wishes she had known how 'empty and degraded' porn would make her feel. 'I wish, too, I'd been told that porn is not reality. It's acting. Most of all, I wish I'd known it can destroy your heart – and your mind.'[10]

These are serious arguments against porn use. And it's bad for others too.

Major damage

Porn is a violation of someone else's sexuality as you choose to look at the person in that way, whether or not he or she is aware of it, or even consenting to it. You have broken into a human being's 'walled garden' where you have no right to be. It may look and seem sweet and enticing, but those fruits and fragrances are not theirs to give away in this way, and not yours to take either.

The porn industry loves to pretend that women, in particular, are happy, consenting adults who have found a way to make a nice buck for themselves. There is much anecdotal evidence that this is untrue, and that many women are coerced, bullied and blackmailed into acts that degrade them – and often leave them damaged physically and mentally.[11]

Then there is the effect on boyfriends and girlfriends, fiancé(e)s, husbands and wives. Matt admits:

> I used to think that using porn was no big deal. After reading the letter my wife wrote about how my porn use made her feel, I now realize that it was basically the same as if I had had a real-life affair or if I'd been with a prostitute, in terms of the damage it caused her and our marriage.[12]

Specialist counsellors in the field of porn and sex addiction report that the effect on 'other halves' is peculiarly devastating, and can be even harder to recover from than an actual affair.[13] It destroys the trust that is at the very heart of sexual intimacy.

It is also a rupture of the intimacy that Christ wants to offer us. We have seen how a high view of human sexual intimacy (which is not everyone's experience, for a range of reasons) points to a higher intimacy with Jesus, the Lover of our souls. Even physical sex at its purest and highest is intended to point us to Christ and the fuller intimacy he wants to share with our souls.

Usurping Christ's rightful place

Our problem is that we try to find other things to take Christ's place. Lovemaking within marriage has profound soothing, exciting, healing and bonding properties, but it can take Christ's place. The subtlety of the Song is that both internally and in the context of the rest of the Bible its message is that sex is not ultimate; only intimacy with Christ is ultimate. Sex outside marriage invariably puts something in Christ's place.[14] And so do porn and sinful masturbation.

How does this work in practice? To simplify things, porn and masturbation provide two things: exciting pleasure and soothing calm. They tend to be used either to relieve or to distract a person from stress, boredom, depression, guilt, fear and a number of other negative states. For example, some people use porn as a distraction from loneliness, as a set of fantasy replacements for romantic disappointment. This seems to be a particular trap for women, though it applies to men too.

Porn can even be used as a kind of reward after a hard day or a hard week.

Managing your mood

Underneath almost all porn use is dysfunctional mood management. We have learned ways of dealing with negative feelings which seem to help us but don't.[15] The problem is that poor mood management habits grow up, becoming increasingly difficult to shake off as they get more and more ingrained in our minds and lives. As the compulsion grows, so does the negative part of the cycle. This is characterized by guilt, shame, self-accusation, self-loathing – and by a feeling that we have driven Christ away (as we have done), our intimacy with him being lost until we repent and receive his forgiveness.

Porn cuts us off from God as we give in to desires that are uncontrolled. In the New Testament, the writer of the letter to the Hebrews advises his readers:

> See that no one is sexually immoral, or is godless like Esau, who for a single meal sold his inheritance rights as the oldest son. Afterwards, as you know, when he wanted to inherit this blessing, he was rejected.
> (Hebrews 12:16–17)

Using porn makes us like Esau who could not control a physical appetite, and was ready to trade his inheritance for short-term pleasure and relief.[16] We enjoy an early taste of our inheritance during this life through our joy in Christ. We lose this when we commit sexual sin of any kind.

What God says

God's guidelines are clear.

1 Your thought life matters to God! Jesus said, 'You have heard that it was said, "You shall not commit adultery." But I tell you that anyone who looks at a woman lustfully has already committed adultery with her in his heart' (Matthew 5:27–28).

So, all porn use is essentially wrong; it is disobeying God's command to be pure and not to think of people you are not married to in sexual fantasies![17]

2 You can learn to control your desires. The apostle Paul addressed this issue in one of his letters:

> It is God's will that you should be sanctified: that you should avoid sexual immorality; that each of you should learn to control your own body in a way that is holy and honourable, not in passionate lust like the pagans, who do not know God . . .
> (1 Thessalonians 4:3–5)

Not ever impossible

Paul insists that Christians can and must control their inner desires. That matches the implications of the Song's warning not to awaken love before its time. We do that by controlling what we look at and what we think about – and our responses to sights we have not necessarily chosen.

If you have read thus far and you are someone who struggles with sin in this area, or is trying to help or live with someone who does, first, well done for following the discussion! This chapter may well have compounded your sense of failure and being trapped. That has been the case with many men I have worked with. It is normal and natural to feel trapped, but it's wrong. You can be free. In the next chapter we will explore how.

Questions

- What has God said to you as you have read this chapter?
- How will you respond?

Prayer

Lord, give me grace to respond to your grace working in me as I have read this chapter. Help me, please, for I cannot do it on my own. Amen.

16

Porn-spoiled lives restored by Christ

The rock group Led Zeppelin wrote a song called 'Heartbreaker' in which a man howls at his sense of betrayal in a relationship – at how his heart has been broken. The most anguished line speaks of the way the woman he adores calls him another man's name when they are making love.[1]

Sexual unfaithfulness is always a heartbreaker and often a marriage-breaker too. The betrayal goes deep.

Spiritual adultery

The Bible describes sin – all sin – within the metaphor of Christ as Lover/Bridegroom/Husband, and us as his beloved/bride/wife. It is spiritual adultery. In James chapter 4 we find people who are in all sorts of verbal knife fights with one another. The author calls them 'adulteresses' (American Standard Version). Their loss of Christian courtesy is a betrayal of Christ's love. James's pastoral concern goes beyond their behaviour: he links it to disordered desires. Their desires ought to be focused on Christ, not merely in obedience, but in appreciation and love.

The Bible uses all sorts of metaphors for sin (becoming unclean, crossing a line, breaking a rule, rebellion, getting lost, being diseased, deadness and many others). The metaphor of sexual unfaithfulness is a particularly powerful and important one, as we saw previously, from the early days of the life of Israel, becoming a torrent of divine complaints and even divine pain in the books of Isaiah, Jeremiah, Ezekiel and, above all, Hosea.

The metaphor of sexual betrayal includes all kinds of sin. Often it refers to worshipping idols, for example. For God, worshipping idols is like a woman calling out another man's name when he tries to make love to her.

That kind of spiritual adultery involves all our sin, which includes our sexual sin and our use of porn. These activities are a betrayal of the intimacy God has given us in Christ. Our desire for what they offer is a desire that should be focused on Christ and his gifts to us. There are divine howls of betrayal.

Restoration

However, that is not the end of the story. The unfaithful wife is invited back. And her unfaithfulness is forgiven. At God's command, Hosea finds that being a prophet means more than explaining God's love. It means, for him, living it in real time in his own life – marrying a prostitute, seeing her become unfaithful, and then, all at God's command, taking her back again:

> The LORD said to me, 'Go, show your love to your wife again, though she is loved by another man and is an adulteress. Love her as the LORD loves the Israelites, though they turn to other gods and love the sacred raisin cakes.'
> (Hosea 3:1)

This is Christ's love for us. He takes us back.

All stained

I bought a new pair of trousers a few years ago in a quaint old shop on a bendy old street right in the middle of Cambridge. As I was paying, I remarked that fresh and new though they were, it would only be a matter of time before black oil from the chain of my bike got on to the legs – impossible to erase.

'Don't worry,' the owner replied. 'Everyone in Cambridge has bike oil on their trouser legs.'

In a fallen world, with fallen sexuality, every single one of us has oil stains on our soul from sexual failure or sin, whether it's physic- ally acted out or something that is merely a sinful fantasy inside. Ray Ortlund comments:

> Sexual sin can be especially devastating, because our sexuality is a profound aspect of our existence. Violating sex is like picking up a highly sophisticated, delicate technological device and using it to hammer nails. In our natural incomprehension, we do not know who we are or how to live. Too soon it's too late. But God gives us our virginity back: 'You were washed, you were sanctified, you were justified in the name of the Lord Jesus Christ and by the Spirit of our God' (1 Corinthians 6:11).[2]

Virginity restored

Here is an extraordinary statement: 'God gives us our virginity back.' Morally and spiritually speaking, we are restored. The unfaithful adulterous wife is made a pure bride: in Isaiah 62:5 it is the unfaithful wife whose virginity has been restored whom the Lord rejoices over and marries. He is the builder who has rebuilt her:

> As a young man marries a young woman,
>   so will your Builder marry you;
> as a bridegroom rejoices over his bride,
>   so will your God rejoice over you.

You can, should and must believe that that is true for you too, and true for all your sin, including your sexual sin and including your use of porn and what you have done as you have looked at it. From a position of defeat and brokenness, God gives you hope and the promise of victory.

A new creation

Ortlund goes on, with great pastoral tenderness, to speak to people broken by their sexual sin and who now find forgiveness:

Sad memories may linger. But they no longer define us, and they are passing away. The truth about us now is this: we are not just patched up versions of what we once were, we are new creations altogether (2 Corinthians 5:17). The new has come. In fact, the new has come back, restoring to us treasures we had once thrown away. God be praised.[3]

This is so important in an era when few couples come to marriage without significant sexual sin. Remember how I quoted a writer who said, 'Untainted virginity is the best wedding gift one can give to a spouse.'[4] But what if you can no longer offer that gift? In Christ, you can offer instead virginity that has been recreated in his grace.

Restoring the overgrown garden

Let's come back to the Song of Songs. Our inner being is like a garden. Humanly speaking, places there are reserved for a husband's or wife's exclusive presence and joy. Spiritually speaking, the garden is a place for Christ to come and find the fruits he loves – openness and receptiveness to his love.

When we sin with porn, we spoil the garden. But he can remake it, fit fresh locks, get rid of the weeds and plant it afresh. If you are in Christ, the garden is being remade. His water is flowing through it and the Gardener is at work – and what a difference he sees! You trashed your garden, but he's replanting it with the flowers that should have been there all along.

Your virginity is restored morally in Christ, and so you're set free to be the kind of sexual being he intended you to be – but, more than that, to be the being he wants you to be in the totality of life. There is this wonderful sense of the deepest part of us becoming a place that is hallowed for Christ himself, so set free to be what it should be, and that makes him happy.

A place he loves

The delight of Christ is to dwell in your inner garden, to see what he has planted growing and flourishing, and to feed on the honeycomb that flows from it and the fruits that are produced there. He touches you at that deep level which actually goes deeper than any of the deep levels.

Sexual partners reach deep joy with each other as their lives are joined together. Christ himself comes in and it gives him great joy. Hear his words of forgiveness, hear his words of recreation, and apply those to your sexual failures as well as to the other failures in your life; realize that this is a portrayal of what your whole life is about. Being a place, a dwelling place, for the Son of God, your Bridegroom, your Husband.

Getting practical

This brings us back to the practicalities of finding freedom from porn and sinful masturbation where we left off at the end of the last chapter.

One man whom I worked with to help him escape a very long-standing porn habit said this:

However much I tried it, the willpower of 'just don't look at it' never worked for me. I could go for a few days, and then the hole left just had to be filled. But then God made me realize that my choice was not simply between looking at porn and not. It was between desiring Jesus who would satisfy or desiring something else which wouldn't. The struggle didn't become easy then, but it did become winnable, because I realized I had to choose not just to walk away from something, but to walk towards Someone.

That is our starting point. To realize that we have been unfaithful to Christ, that we have betrayed him, that we have sought pleasure and release in the wrong place, not in him and the means he gives us. We need to admit these things, walking towards him, not away, receiving his forgiveness and opening ourselves to what he wants to do to set us free. Here is a list to help you or whoever you are helping. I have drawn on my own experience of counselling others and from the wisdom of the plentiful resources now available in this area.

1 Disclosure

Talk to someone suitable. Yes, people do become porn-free on their own, but not many. Almost all need help from another person, so the first step is to tell someone suitable. Two experts in this area make this comment: '"I have a problem with porn and I want to quit." When a porn user first says words like these out loud to another person, he takes a significant first step in climbing out of the porn trap.'[5]

They go on to say: 'Former porn users ... were passionate about the importance of self-disclosure in breaking free of a porn addiction.'[6]

2 Abstinence

Before you take that step of starting to abstain from using porn, it might feel as though you need to do a hundred and one other things first. The problem is that porn can get such a grip on our minds that it creates a kind of fog there. Set yourself a target of a minimum of sixty days and start right now.

3 Education

Read about the way porn works, how it creates dependent and even addictive habits. Many people find it helpful to understand the cycles of behaviour that are typical.

4 Analysis

Look at your habits. When are you vulnerable? Why? What circumstances make porn possible? Work it out and be specific.

5 Action on opportunity and access

Remember how Jesus talks of taking drastic action with sexual sin:

> If your right eye causes you to stumble, gouge it out and throw it away. It is better for you to lose one part of your body than for your whole body to be thrown into hell.

And if your right hand causes you to stumble, cut it off and throw it away. It is better for you to lose one part of your body than for your whole body to go into hell.
(Matthew 5:29–30)

Work out your access points to porn and take drastic action in order to deal with them.

One man whom I worked with tended to watch sexually explicit material in period dramas on the BBC iPlayer website. So, he had to admit this to his wife and let her control the password for the account. Another knew that certain apps on his phone were dangerous for him, so he gave a friend control of the password for installing new apps. Another started leaving his laptop at the office (where he knew he was unlikely to watch porn) rather than taking it home (where he might). There are all sorts of things that we can do to limit access.

Many find accountability software a good deterrent or a way of alerting accountability partners to a lapse.

These different actions will all tend to feel irksome, may mean embarrassing conversations, and will feel like cutting something off that belongs to you. Do them anyway!

6 Accountability

Find at least two trusted accountability partners.

At least one needs to be someone older than you and not already using *you* as an accountability partner: too many try to manage with reciprocal peer accountability, using a friend who has the same struggles, and too often they simply end up excusing each other's failures. You need a spiritual senior whom you trust – a pastor, church worker, house group leader, mentor.

Then have peer accountability with one other person or perhaps a group (which can be very powerful).

7 Action on mood management

All approaches to porn addiction point to the importance of better mood management, as this is the heart of the problem.

- Jason feels anxious and seeks out porn to distract him.
- Mary is feeling happy but tired after a successful week at work. She looks online for something that will give her that little bit of extra reward that she deserves.
- Frank is just miserable and bored. Life seems so grey on Saturdays. He opens up a book with some explicit sexual description in it to find a kind of pleasure life denies him.

Non-Christians and Christians alike need to find better ways of managing their moods, whether bad or even good. This means alternative ways of finding soothing, distraction or even joy.

- Jason needs to learn a better way of dealing with his anxiety.
- Mary needs to find an alternative reward or settle for the sense of accomplishment that she has already.
- For Frank, Saturdays are clearly a tricky time, so he would do well to plan some colour for them.

Learning to live with less than perfection

The more insightful approaches don't only try to fill holes or replace pain, but give us ways of living with boredom, emptiness and anxiety. Jenni Russell wrote in *The Times* that we are too often miserable because of unrealistic expectations:

Alain de Botton's *The School of Life: An Emotional Education* is here to remind us that life is made up of constant and inevitable dissatisfactions, that all humans are muddled, inconsistent, difficult to understand and intrinsically flawed, and that our contemporary belief that it's possible to be enduringly happy is a destructive myth that's driving us to collective rage. What de Botton hopes to free us from is the tyranny of expecting perfection, happiness or fairness to be our due, to accept that melancholy and disappointment are natural and inevitable, to take delight in lives that are good enough, with moments of joy. We should cultivate realism, humour, forgiveness and politeness as essential virtues.[7]

There is great wisdom here, not just about our sexuality, but also about our careers and families and holidays. We should not neglect the practical tactics which both believers and non-believers can use to achieve change (for example, a workout at the gym rather than masturbating, or ten to fifteen minutes of deep slow breathing rather than searching for stuff online).

Above all, Christ

However, the greatest power and the holiest approach is found in seeking more intimacy with Christ. Our porn habit is spiritual adultery – seeking pleasure, distraction, soothing and love in the wrong places. Jesus is remaking our inner garden. He himself wants to come into that garden repeatedly, especially when it feels cold and empty and grey. He wants to come in to give us himself in tender, personal and passionate love. That is where the spaces and emptiness help us.

Our experience of anxiety feels ghastly, but it is Christ showing us that we can't make it on our own so that we will turn to him. No one, but no one, likes feeling lonely. But Christ changes loneliness into a solitude with him. Again and again, I have talked with widowed people in their nineties and asked them about their lives. Again and again, they have told me about an enhanced sense of the living presence of their Lover, Christ; sometimes they have said this almost forcefully, as if it was of course the case.

8 Refuse to give up hope

Here are some encouragements:

Hank: 'For 30 years from the time I started using porn compulsively until I hit bottom with it, I was completely unsatisfied, undeveloped and unhappy as a human being. Since I quit porn three years ago, my whole life has changed.'[8]

Mitch: 'I feel spiritually renewed. My life is no longer a contradiction.'[9]

It will be worth it, and you can have this freedom and victory. I could point you to many guys I have worked with for whom porn is no longer a part of their lives. It can be the same for you.

There is no hole so deep and dark that sinful hearts won't fall into it if we let them. There is no hole so deep and dark that Christ can't reach down and lift us out if we ask him. He is recreating the ruined garden of your soul.

Questions

- What in this chapter has spoken to your life right now?
- If you yourself are not currently using porn or sinful masturbation, how does it speak to you about other dysfunctional and sinful patterns in your life?
- How can the insights here help you with friends who may be struggling in these areas?
- Why is it important to use more than just willpower to escape sinful habits?

Resources

There are many helpful books on this subject, including:

- Tim Chester, *Captured by a Better Vision: Living porn-free* (IVP, 2010);
- Heath Lambert, *Finally Free: Fighting for purity with the power of grace* (Zondervan, 2013);
- Paula Hall, *Confronting Porn* (Naked Truth Resources, 2016).

The Naked Truth Project is helpful in many ways: <http://thenakedtruthproject.com>.

17

Reconciliation: back together again

Andrew had been rude and insensitive to Francesca. She had wanted to start Saturday morning slowly and tenderly in bed, getting up late, going out for an almond croissant and flat white coffee in the café, talking through the preceding week's ups and downs and starting to plan their summer holiday.

He had jumped out of bed at the usual time and gone into the garden to get going on his latest grand project, a tree house for their nephews and nieces. She tried to call him in, but she thought he just grunted at her. Eventually, she had had enough and went into town on her own to meet a friend at a new coffee shop they hadn't tried.

As it happened, Andrew's grunt was actually a reply that said 'Sure, be with you in a minute'. But as he was wearing a face mask to keep out the sawdust, she hadn't heard it. He came in, washed his hands and headed expectantly upstairs, but their bedroom was empty.

'Francesca, where are you?' he called.

No reply.

It wasn't a huge house, so quite quickly he realized she had gone out. He even looked in the cupboard under the stairs and the carport, in case she was playing a game of hide and seek. Reaching for his phone, he texted her: *I'm here.*

No reply.

Frannie, waiting for you!

No reply.

He left it a few minutes and had a shower to remove the sawdust properly from his hair. *Hi Fran, I'm at home . . .*

No reply.

Where are you, darling?

No reply.

He got out his bike and cycled to their favourite coffee shop. Plenty of people enjoying a leisurely Saturday morning, including, he noticed, a number of irritatingly lovey-dovey couples who all seemed to be having a happy time. No Francesca. He asked the barista, 'Have you seen a woman about my age, tall, strawberry blonde, bit skinny, probably wearing a stripey blue top?'

'No, sorry.'

He was starting to alternate between irritation and concern. *Where ARE you?*

No reply.

He looked at her icon on the app and saw that she had last used it at 9.30 am – just about the time she had left the house. He went on a long cycle ride around town looking for her. Every few minutes he stopped to check his phone – and to send another text message.

Hello . . . ?

Can you just tell me where you are?

Where on earth ARE you?

Frannie?

The phone went, but it was a person pretending to be from his bank. What made it worse was that his ring tone had cycled round to 'You've Lost That Lovin' Feeling' by The Righteous Brothers.

At lunchtime he swallowed his pride and sent another message, this time to her friend. *Mel, I can't find Frannie. Do you know where she is?*

No reply.

If you see her can you tell her I love her?

An hour later, that did produce a reply from Mel: *What is it about Frannie that makes her special to you?*

You've disappeared

We left the woman in the Song of Songs rather like Andrew in this made-up story, calling 'Where are you?' Sometimes when we rebuff Christ's approach, he allows us to find him again quite quickly.

Sometimes he is more elusive. This feels like one of those more elusive times.

She needs help, so she turns to her friends:

Daughters of Jerusalem, I charge you –
 if you find my beloved,
what will you tell him?
 Tell him I am faint with love.
(Song 5:8)

You can't make it on your own

Both in human relationships and in our relationship with Christ it can be so useful to ask for help. When the problem is with another person, this will need care and discretion. With Christ, talking with another Christian is very often the key to progress, as he or she may have wisdom and insight that we lack. It is interesting in the Song that the friends don't give the young woman advice. They ask her questions. They do remind her in passing that she is the most beautiful of women, which presumably means most beautiful to *him*, but the main thing they do is ask questions. That is often the best way to help someone. The questions draw out the woman's appreciation of her lover:

How is your beloved better than others,
 most beautiful of women?
How is your beloved better than others,
 that you so charge us?
(Song 5:9)

The friends invite her to bring him to mind and to think about all his qualities: the beauty of his physical appearance, the character qualities that amuse and impress her, the reasons why she is drawn and attracted to him. At the human level, if we are feeling negative about someone, this is a telling exercise! Spiritually, it is powerful and important too.

The woman throws herself into it, pouring out a stream of accolades, using the mixed collage of pictures we are getting used to in the Song, some of them strange to our eyes today:

My beloved is radiant and ruddy,
    outstanding among ten thousand.
His head is purest gold;
    his hair is wavy
    and black as a raven.
His eyes are like doves
    by the water streams,
washed in milk,
    mounted like jewels.
His cheeks are like beds of spice
    yielding perfume.
His lips are like lilies
    dripping with myrrh.
His arms are rods of gold
    set with topaz.
His body is like polished ivory
    decorated with lapis lazuli.
His legs are pillars of marble
    set on bases of pure gold.
His appearance is like Lebanon,
    choice as its cedars.
His mouth is sweetness itself;
    he is altogether lovely.
This is my beloved, this is my friend,
    daughters of Jerusalem.
(Song 5:10–16)

It's almost as though she's creating a picture of the most amazing statue. Gold signifies rarity and riches and preciousness. He has a kind of loving aroma about him that she loves to savour. He is strong but tender. You could not shake him off his feet easily, but when he opens his mouth it is so gentle. The great summary is that, to her, he's outstanding among ten thousand or ten million others. To her, he is simply the best.

Jesus is uniquely beautiful. Here is an experienced pastor's monumental effort to explain how:

> He is the woman's seed crushing Satan, the Passover Lamb, the High Priest entering heaven for his people, the pillar of cloud and fire, the Prophet greater than Moses, the Captain of our salvation, the perfect King, the One who rebuilds broken walls, the Saviour, the Lord and Shepherd, the Lover and Bridegroom, the Son of Man who is with us in the fire, the longsuffering Husband, the One who pours out his Spirit, the One who bears our burdens, the Messenger with beautiful feet, the Restorer of God's lost heritage, the King who brings peace and humbly rides on a colt, the Son of Righteousness risen with healing in his wings.
>
> He is the Friend who sticks closer than a brother, the One greater than all, whose blood washes away sin, the Great Shepherd and Bishop of our souls, everlasting Lover, the Keeper of our souls, the Lamb that was slain and the Lion of Judah, the King of kings and Lord of lords.[1]

When we lived in Chicago, we were taken aback at first by how obsessed the city was with the sport of basketball and with the local professional team, the Chicago Bulls. Our last year there saw the start of the second phase of the glory days of one of the greatest basketball players there has ever been, Michael Jordan. Funnily enough, he lived on our street: he was at number 22, and we (and many others on the seminary and college campus) were at 2065 Half-Day Road. We even managed to go and see Jordan (and the rest of the Bulls) play once or twice, and it was some experience.

Outside the great arena that was built in downtown Chicago (essentially to showcase Jordan), there's a statue of him, about one-and-a-half times life size (and he is a big man). Around three sides of the plinth his achievements are listed – not only the championships he won but also his individual totals and averages for points, steals, rebounds and assists. People who know tell me that these are exceedingly impressive. On the fourth side of the plinth there's a caption:

The best there ever was
The best there ever will be

This may well be true of Jordan the basketball player. But it is absolutely true of Jesus Christ. He is the best there ever was. He is the best there ever will be. He is the fairest of ten thousand. We will never find anywhere else or anyone else where there is such love, such beauty. We need to be convinced of that, especially if we have been cool towards him.

As we see it again, we are invited to say, 'This is my beloved; this is my friend.' Think about it. Could you tell someone why Christ is uniquely precious to you?

The woman's friends speak again. They ask her another question, designed to make her attend to what has happened:

Where has your beloved gone,
    most beautiful of women?
Which way did your beloved turn,
    that we may look for him with you?
(Song 6:1)

It is as if the question makes her realize what has happened:

My beloved has gone down to his garden,
    to the beds of spices,
to browse in the gardens
    and to gather lilies.
(Song 6:2)

This is picture language. She is the garden (4:12); she is the spices (4:14). Going into the garden is a discreet way of saying that he is with her in love (5:1). She realizes that she's back with him. He is enjoying her and enjoying her presence. There is pleasure for him in their reunion as he browses among the lilies. All she can say is:

I am my beloved's and my beloved is mine;
    he browses among the lilies.
(Song 6:3)

She gives herself to him eagerly because to her he is the best. And he finds his desire met in her yielding. Again, we remember what is at the heart of the beloved/bride/wife image: receptiveness to the Lover/Bridegroom/Husband.

Recalling Jesus

It would be rather artificial to say that this is a set pattern for finding Christ again when he seems far away. It is one poem, with one imagined event. But it does point us to what may be helpful. Thinking again about why Jesus is precious reminds us that he is better than any alternative centre for our lives.

A married person wrote:

Jesus passionately desires intimacy with me, and my own sexual desire truly finds its answer in knowing him – [these] ideas which for me were fresh . . . have enriched my walk with Jesus. As a married person, the series [of sermons] has made a significant difference both in my relationship with my wife, but also in understanding the limitations of marriage and sex and allowing them to point me to satisfaction in Christ.

It also reminds us that he is infinitely forgiving: we may have blanked him in the street, but he will meet our eyes with his gaze of love and say 'I forgive you' again and again and again. As we surrender to him, he will be like the husband in the poem because he will be finding *his* desires fulfilled by what he sees in us. Our wanting to want him will bring him great joy, like the deer grazing among the lilies.

Joy in the end

The poet and hymnwriter William Cowper (whom we met earlier) struggled on and on with his melancholy and his doubts. On his deathbed something happened:

> Cowper lay in extreme weakness, dying; there had not come to him one gleam of hope, and now he was without power to speak. John Johnson his nephew was watching by him, and with thoughts strongly tempted towards a blank infidelity, by the sight of such goodness seemingly so deserted. But now, on a sudden, there came a change. The dying face was irradiated as with a surprise of joy, 'unspeakable and full of glory'. William Cowper lay speechless, motionless, but enraptured, for the last half-hour before the ceasing of his breath. Then did the nephew clasp the dead man's Bible to his heart, saying, 'His faith shall be my faith, and his God shall be my God.'[2]

What pleasure Christ must have taken in that!

Question

- If Christ seems distant to you right now, could it help you to think about how special he is?

Prayer

Lord, forgive me for ever thinking that anything or anyone could match you. Thank you that you are simply the Best. Amen.

18

Still beautiful
after all these years

My favourite film is *Chariots of Fire*. I remember seeing it when it first came out in 1982 in a double bill (whatever happened to those?) with *Gregory's Girl*, a very different film but in its own way equally classic. My fellow gap-year friends and I got the number 8 bus from Dalston Lane in Hackney to a plush cinema in the West End of London, full of anticipation based on the early reviews. We were not disappointed.

Here is a brief summary of *Chariots of Fire*. It is based on the true story of two British sprinters who compete in the Paris Olympics of 1924. Both have special hurdles to overcome.

Harold Abrahams is Jewish and encounters some of the anti-Semitic prejudice rife in British society at that time. He hires a professional coach, which elicits all sorts of disapproving intakes of breath. He wins the 100 metres.

The second sprinter is Eric Liddell, a Scot, a Christian called by God to be an evangelist and a missionary. The hurdles for Liddell are the conflict between a life of athletic competition, with the success it promises, and his calling to follow Christ. At the micro level, this comes to a head when the semi-final of his favoured event is scheduled for a Sunday. Liddell, as a Sabbatarian, believes athletic competition on a Sunday to be breaking God's command. In the end, he is able to enter another event, which he wins.

My favourite moment comes a little earlier in the film, when he discusses with his sister his decision about both running and overseas mission work. First, he tells her that he is going to go to China (where they had both been born to missionary parents). She is ecstatic. Then he adds that, before leaving, he is also going to compete in the Olympics. This impresses her rather less. He tries to explain: 'God made me to be fast, and when I run, I feel his pleasure.'

There is no evidence that the real Eric Liddell ever spoke those words. A scriptwriter put them into his mouth. But he could have done! They are theologically spot on.

A few years ago I went into a Christian bookshop and saw a book I hadn't heard of previously. As soon as I saw the title, I thought to myself: I'm going to have that book, whatever it costs. The title was *The Pleasures of God*.[1]

God feels pleasure

Up to that point the idea of God having *pleasures* was not something that had occurred to me, so I thought it would be fascinating to see what it meant. In fact, it turned out to be more than fascinating; it was totally gripping and absorbing, and transforming, like realizing that a new garden had a tree that produced delicious fruit every summer.

The chapter titles describe the pleasure of God:

- in his Son;
- in all he does;
- in his creation;
- in his fame;
- in election;
- in bruising his Son;
- in doing good to all who hope in him;
- in the prayers of the upright;
- in personal obedience;
- in public justice.

The book is well worth reading, and it could also have many more chapters added. This section of the Song represents one of them: the pleasure of God in the beauty of his people, collectively and individually:

You are as beautiful as Tirzah, my darling,
  as lovely as Jerusalem,
  as majestic as troops with banners.
Turn your eyes from me;
  they overwhelm me.
Your hair is like a flock of goats
  descending from Gilead.
Your teeth are like a flock of sheep
  coming up from the washing.
Each has its twin,
  not one of them is missing.
Your temples behind your veil
  are like the halves of a pomegranate.
Sixty queens there may be,
  and eighty concubines,
  and virgins beyond number;
but my dove, my perfect one, is unique,
  the only daughter of her mother,
  the favourite of the one who bore her.
The young women saw her and called her blessed;
  the queens and concubines praised her.
(Song 6:4–9)

Much of this will sound familiar because it repeats a number of phrases from a similar passage in Song chapter 4. This is deliberate. She has brushed him off. He has withdrawn. She has come out to find him. They are back together. He has the emotional intelligence to know that she needs him to reaffirm his love for her and his appreciation of her beauty.

Full of excitement, he tells her that he is still crazy about her, using the same extraordinary comparisons – goats, sheep, pomegranates:

Your hair is like a flock of goats
  descending from Gilead.
Your teeth are like a flock of sheep
  coming up from the washing.

Each has its twin,
> not one of them is missing.
Your temples behind your veil
> are like the halves of a pomegranate.
(Song 6:5b–7)

The effect is powerful. Using language that is new, he suggests he may now be crazier in love than ever:

Turn your eyes from me;
> they overwhelm me.
(Song 6:5a)

Charles Spurgeon will not let us avoid the implication of this. He insists: 'The eyes of Christ's chosen ones still overcome him.'[2]

Special and beautiful to him

The lover adds in a few new thoughts as though to say that he now sees new things about his beloved that are beautiful to him. As before, he wants to stress how uniquely special she is to him:

Sixty queens there may be,
> and eighty concubines,
> and virgins beyond number;
but my dove, my perfect one, is unique,
> the only daughter of her mother,
> the favourite of the one who bore her.
The young women saw her and called her blessed;
> the queens and concubines praised her.
(Song 6:8–9)

It is an expression of the pleasure of Christ, the Lover of our souls, in us, his beloved. We come back to the same idea for the third or fourth time in the Song. This is no accident. God does not intend us to be like tourists going round Paris who find themselves outside the

Louvre yet again but refuse to go in because they have already had an afternoon there. He wants us to retread the same path of this theme – and enjoy it even more!

I have a feeling that readers who still find it hard to believe that this is biblical may find it helpful to look at some supportive biblical data. This idea of Christ rejoicing over the beauty of his redeemed people starts in the Old Testament:

> As a young man marries a young woman,
>   so will your Builder marry you;
> as a bridegroom rejoices over his bride,
>   so will your God rejoice over you.
> (Isaiah 62:5)

In church history many writers have taken up this idea and presented it movingly. I wonder if you remember Martin Luther's great statement which we looked at earlier: 'The grace of God does not find but creates what is pleasing to him.'

Luther returns to this elsewhere: 'When faith in Christ is present, he is delighted at my beauty which he himself has conferred on me.' And he applies it: 'Therefore I ought not to doubt that I am altogether lovely for the sake of Christ.' 'Do you doubt it? Stop doubting and believe!' says the fiery German ex-monk.[3]

He says in another place: 'Christ our King takes pleasure not only in the Word and faith but he is stirred and transported towards us such as a bridegroom is for his bride that he spontaneously pursues us.'[4]

Luther wrote about this at more length at the height of the bruising encounters that followed his posting of the 'Ninety-Five Theses' in Wittenburg in October 1517:

Faith unites the soul with Christ like a bride with a bridegroom. By this mystery Christ and the soul are made one flesh . . . [so] they hold all things in common. Who can even begin to appreciate this royal marriage? Here, this rich upstanding bridegroom, Christ, marries this poor disloyal little prostitute, redeems her from all evil and adorns her with all his goodness. For, now it is impossible for her sins to destroy her because they have been laid upon Christ and devoured by him.

In Christ her bridegroom, she has her righteousness, which she can enjoy as her very own property. And with confidence she can set this righteousness over against all her sins and in opposition to death and hell and say: 'Sure I have sinned, but my Christ, whom I trust, has not sinned. All that is his is mine and all that is mine is his.'[5]

Jonathan Edwards picks up this idea and draws on remarkable words in 2 Peter 1:4 – that we are enabled to 'participate in the divine nature' through trusting the 'very great and precious promises' God has given us:

Christian living is participation in God, in 'the supreme loveliness of his nature'. And if what defines God supremely is his beauty or loveliness or excellency, then to participate in the triune life of God is to be swept up into, and to exude, that heavenly resplendence. A Christian is one who is being beautified.[6]

And Christ sees that! He finds you beautiful. He really does. You may still be saying, 'How can that be?' We can edge closer to that experience if we open ourselves to hear him say, 'You are beautiful, my love' (Song 1:15 ESV).

We are beautiful to him because he has not kept back any of this beauty from us.

All that is mine . . .

I have a friend whose wife left him for a fellow member of their tennis club and started divorce proceedings. It was so sad. A few years later he met another woman and became engaged. I was delighted to be able to go to their engagement party, which was a lively occasion. My friend made a moving speech in which he thanked a number of people who had helped him in different ways. One of them was his brother.

He explained that in the difficult week when the divorce papers were served, his brother phoned him in support. He realized that divorce would mean considerable financial pressure for my friend because of existing commitments that could only be cancelled at the expense of his children's well-being. The brother said, 'But I don't want you to worry, because I want you to know that all I have is yours.'

That is what Christ says to us: 'All I have is yours.' And a wonderful part of that is the conferral of his beauty on us, transforming our ugliness and fear. To quote Dane Ortlund again: 'The Christian is a mini-advertisement for divine beauty. To be a Christian is to be a little, frail, finite, morally faltering picture of the beauty of God.'[7]

That is certainly true for Eric Liddell. He went on to win a gold medal (in a world-record time) for the 400-metre race. He also went out to China, where he served as a missionary for many years. During the Second World War his part of China was captured by the Japanese army. Liddell was captured and, with many others, lived in a Japanese prison camp where conditions were appallingly hard. Jack Cotterill, a fellow missionary, who was a close friend of Liddell's, was there with him. His account of this stage of Liddell's life is reported by Duncan Hamilton:

As Weihsien [camp] deteriorated in every way, and the war ground on seemingly without end, internees who had led blameless lives began openly to question both their religious faith and the overall purpose of the Church. Some asked Liddell directly, 'What is the point of continuing to pray – for food, for comfort, for rescue – when those prayers aren't being answered?' Where was God? Why wasn't He listening? Also, why had He 'allowed' Weihsien to happen in the first place? Hearing him recite his daily devotions, Cotterill knew not only that Liddell's own belief never wavered, but also that he reassured those who had doubts.

'His faith grew stronger than ever in such troubled times,' he said. 'He didn't blame God for the situation we were all in. He believed God was in that situation with us. That was his message, and he never stopped preaching it. He'd say to us all, "Have faith."'

Liddell regularly read aloud from the Sermon on the Mount and dwelt on one passage: 'Love your enemies. Bless them that curse you. Do good to them that hate you. Pray for them which despitefully use you and persecute you.'

Early in 1944 he began urging the internees to pray specific- ally for the men in uniform – the camp guards. Liddell told his congregation and also his Sunday school classes: 'I've begun to pray for the guards and it's changed my whole attitude towards them. When we hate them, we are self-centred.'[8]

If God took pleasure in his running, in his winning the gold medal in unusual circumstances in the 400-metre race in the Paris 1924 Olympics, how much more did God take pleasure in the beauty of Jesus Christ worked through directly in the mature life of Liddell in that prison camp? With an imaginative leap of faith, we see for a moment Christ's perspective and his pleasure in the beauty of Christ in Eric Liddell.

The danger of these kinds of illustrations is that they seem slightly unreal, especially if we focus on the highly unlikely scenario of winning a gold medal in the Olympics. Even the war and prison camps are far from our everyday experience. But think for a moment of being in a tough situation where people are treating you badly, and/or where there are other Christians who are not finding it easy to hold on to Christ in faith. That's something which is open to any of us, and will be the case for many.

We should never imagine, whatever phase, whatever difficulties, whatever hardship in life we're in, that this is not a moment when Christ doesn't want more of us, and when Christ can't grow his own beauty in us, and find us beautiful.

Some years ago the rock group Radiohead released a poignant, mournful track called 'Fake Plastic Trees'. It is about that sense, in a relationship, of being expected to be something you aren't, and how exhausting that is. The singer tries to be the kind of person his lover wants, but it just wears him out.[9]

Many people feel like that about their relationship with Christ. They find it very hard to believe that they are forgiven, and almost impossible to believe that he could find them beautiful. He comes to us in the Song of Songs and tells us that we are his and he desires us.

One person in our church, who had not previously thought much about Christ's delight in us, came upon this idea and was deeply affected:

Understanding that Christ delights in us as his bride is an enormously enriching and encouraging truth, which catches the soul up to worship in response. It is not a truth which we dwell on as often as we should, but is a thoroughly biblical theme. Personally, my prayer life has been deeply affected by recognizing God's delight in us and in our prayers – a wonderful motivation to pray!

Questions

- Is it hard for you to believe that God finds you beautiful in Christ?
- If so, why?
- Why not ask Christ to use one of these images of his delight in you to make you more aware of his love?

Prayer

Lord, you are beauty itself, and beyond all my wildest dreams you find me beautiful. Not in myself, but in yourself. It's hard to understand, Lord, let alone experience. But I want to open myself up to both. What do I need to do, Lord? And what do you need to do? Amen.

19

The spiral staircase of longing and love

James Joyce wrote a novel called *Finnegans Wake*.[1] I am afraid I've never read it, but I do know that it is a strange book, opening in the middle of a sentence and finishing with the first half of that same sentence. In other words, it is circular, a never-ending circle of, well, whatever *Finnegans Wake* is about.

Back to the start

The Song of Songs has little else in common with *Finnegans Wake*, but at the end it too seems to return to its starting point. Why would it do this? To point to the perpetual cycle of love. The ending of the Song is not the wedding night of chapters 4 and 5, but this invitation from the woman to the man:

> Come away, my beloved,
>   and be like a gazelle
> or like a young stag
>   on the spice-laden mountains.
> (Song 8:14)

This is a direct echo of 2:17, but thematically it pushes us right back to the beginning of the book and her saying how much she wants to kiss him:

> Let him kiss me with the kisses of his mouth –
>   for your love is more delightful than wine.
> (Song 1:2)

All about desire

People generally think that the main theme of the Song of Songs is sex. As I have studied it, I have realized that the main theme is actually desire, the human longing for something or someone. The song portrays the cycles of desire and fulfilment which make up married life, and indeed all human life. We are never static. As soon as we have had a really good meal, we start again on a cycle in which we will feel hungry – and we can't eat memories!

Repeated cycles

The same is true of friendship and marriage, including physical intimacy. All relationships have cycles in which we move closer, then necessarily move away, and then draw closer again. Old Testament lecturer Richard Hess explains it this way (quoting another Old Testament lecturer Dianne Bergant):

> 'Human love knows no definitive consummation, no absolute fulfillment. Loving relationships are never complete. They are always ongoing, always reaching out for more. Regardless of the quality or frequency of lovemaking, there is always a measure of yearning present.' The finitude of human love points toward something greater and more complete.[2]

The love that Christ has for us, the love that we know now in our relationship with the Lord Jesus, also goes in cycles. It is a repeated experience of desiring God, of realizing that we're dry and we need to be drenched, realizing that we're spiritually hungry and need to be fed, realizing that we're distracted and we need to be focused, realizing that we're frazzled and need to be given his peace. This creates an endless cycle that continues through life.

Knowing Christ in the here and now is one of the highest Christian experiences. But it is incomplete. The apostle Peter writes to believers in the early church: 'Though you have not seen him, you love him; and even though you do not see him now, you believe in him and are filled with an inexpressible and glorious joy' (1 Peter 1:8).

The readers of the letter have not seen Jesus, but they love him. They cannot see him, but they believe in him, and that faith brings them a quite extraordinary joy. Peter says it is 'inexpressible'. It goes beyond words.

Surpassing an idea

Paul describes this experience as 'knowing the love that surpasses knowledge' (see Ephesians 3:19). It is knowing the unknowable – a knowing that goes beyond verbal propositions about God and gospel into the reality they describe. We read a review of a new album – classical or rock – and then hear the music. If it is a good review, nothing in the listening will contradict the text of the review; nevertheless, reading about music is just not the same thing as hearing it.

It is the difference between love letters and physical lovemaking: one is propositional; the other is the aim and consummation of all that has been written, but it surpasses verbal definition without in any way contradicting it. John Murray has expressed this well:

> It is necessary for us to recognize that there is an intelligent mysticism in the life of faith . . . of living union and communion with the exalted and ever-present Redeemer . . . he communes with his people and his people commune with him in conscious reciprocal love . . . The life of true faith cannot be that of cold metallic assent. It must have the passion and warmth of love and communion because communion with God is the crown and apex of true religion.[3]

A loving relationship with Christ is deeply personal and totally real. And it is based on him looking at you and experiencing pleasure – and you, by faith, feeling that pleasure, as Eric Liddell did, not just in his running but in all of his life as it was offered to Jesus.

More to come

A crucial pastoral impact of the Song in its detail and its totality is to stir up desire for more of Christ. Much of this life is about desiring him – and some of it is about that desire being met in delight in the present. But just as the best things this world has to offer point to another world, we should not think that we can experience all he has to offer at once or in this life. It is right to desire him and to find delight in him, and also to find our desire returning because there is much more we have not yet experienced.

Thus, in Song of Songs 7:1–9 we read fresh words of appreciation revealing how the man feels for his beloved:

Song 7:1　How beautiful your sandalled feet,
　　　　　O prince's daughter!
　　　　　Your graceful legs are like jewels,
　　　　　the work of an artist's hands.

Song 7:2　Your navel is a rounded goblet
　　　　　that never lacks blended wine.
　　　　　Your waist is a mound of wheat
　　　　　encircled by lilies.

Song 7:3　Your breasts are like two fawns,
　　　　　like twin fawns of a gazelle.

Song 7:4　Your neck is like an ivory tower.
　　　　　Your eyes are the pools of Heshbon
　　　　　by the gate of Bath Rabbim.
　　　　　Your nose is like the tower of Lebanon
　　　　　looking towards Damascus.

Song 7:5　Your head crowns you like Mount Carmel.
　　　　　Your hair is like royal tapestry;
　　　　　the king is held captive by its tresses.

Song 7:6　How beautiful you are and how pleasing,
　　　　　my love, with your delights!

Song 7:7　Your stature is like that of the palm,
　　　　　and your breasts like clusters of fruit.

Song 7:8   I said, 'I will climb the palm tree;
             I will take hold of its fruit.'
             May your breasts be like clusters of grapes on the
             vine,
             the fragrance of your breath like apples,
Song 7:9a and your mouth like the best wine.

There are echoes here of what the man has said before, and there are new pictures and expressions. We see the same mixture of delight and desire.

We also hear the woman's response, yielding willingly and hungrily to him:

Song 7:9b May the wine go straight to my beloved,
             flowing gently over lips and teeth.
Song 7:10 I belong to my beloved,
             and his desire is for me.
Song 7:11 Come, my beloved, let us go to the countryside,
             let us spend the night in the villages.
Song 7:12 Let us go early to the vineyards
             to see if the vines have budded,
             if their blossoms have opened,
             and if the pomegranates are in bloom –
             there I will give you my love.

As we have seen so often, metaphors and reality blur (is it a country retreat they are going to, or is that itself a metaphor? And does it matter?). What is very clear is the anticipation of pleasure. She responds enticingly, 'The mandrakes send out their fragrance ...' This is enticing for him because mandrakes were regarded as love fruits.[4] But what follows is almost unencoded:

     ... and at our door is every delicacy,
  both new and old,
     that I have stored up for you, my beloved.
(Song 7:13)

The discreet description of intimacy as 'every delicacy, both new and old' shows that the cycles of desire and love are not static.

Cycles and spirals

This pictures for us the cycles of our relationship with Christ. He continues to appreciate us and wants us to long for him. He wants us to continue to feel more desire for him again, yield to him and experience his closeness again.

The problem with the word 'cycles' is that it could imply doing exactly the same thing over and over again. Near my house is a sports field. It is a lovely open green space. The perimeter is about 600 metres. I know because I have run round it. Repeatedly. Once I completed 15 kilometres, which would be twenty-five laps, every single one more or less the same as the last. My wife thinks I am mad to run that much, and madder still to run it in circles. I suspect that it doesn't sound terribly appealing. But that is not the kind of cycle the Song imagines for married, sexual or spiritual intimacy.

It is more like spiral paths going gently round and round a splendid mountain. As you pause to look at the view to the south-west, it looks even better on the second spiral than it did an hour ago and from 400 metres directly below. At the jutting-out 'corner' looking north-west, a spring tumbles down the mountain. The higher you go, the cooler and more refreshing it becomes. One slope getting a lot of sun is particularly rich in fruit trees and bushes, but it feels that as you move higher and hit it again, the higher fruits are even better than the last ones, every time. This continues through life.

Our relationship with Christ is variable in this life. We go through cycles of being closer to him, being less close to him, feeling more of him, feeling less of him, and so on, but this also points us beyond. Ellen Davis has said: 'God never fully satisfies us in this world, but instead constantly stretches our desire toward heaven. Not satisfaction, but the expansion of holy desire is the surest proof of God's presence with us.'[5]

In other words, it's not just about feeling spiritually great. It's about wanting more and more and more, and being aware of the gap.

Learning to realize that you are thirsting for more of Christ. Letting Christ himself do whatever it takes to clear the space for more of him. The repeated experience of the exposure and removal of deep piles of rubbish in this life is the deep working of God in your soul, designed to make you long for more than this life can offer. These, the great earlier spiritual writers have pointed out, are the marks of the Holy Spirit, creating that longing for more. Davis comments: 'The art of the spiritual life is the art of learning to live with longing, with the eager expectation that God's presence will be felt yet again in our hearts, in our midst, and always in new ways.'[6]

We do this with the realistic knowledge that we will never fully know Christ until we meet him in glory. We have to harness that sense of longing, harness that sense of absence, to drive us on to open ourselves up more to him, to receive what he wants to give us in any particular moment or phase of our lives. This, in turn, will push us outside ourselves in the fierce love of service to God and to others in this life until we meet him in the perfect intimacy of the next life.

Questions

- If you are currently feeling a bit spiritually dry, might that mean that Christ is wanting to stir up fresh desires for more of himself?
- If, at present, you are full of joy, would it help to realize that to experience more joy, you may need to receive the gift of a little emptiness?

Prayers

Lord, some of the blessedness has faded a bit. Will you lead me into fresh joy? Amen.

Lord, it is wonderful to be so close to you. If this present moment dims, stir up my longing for even more of you next time. Amen.

20

Love is stronger than death

Bishop Mike Curry of the Episcopal Church of America preached on the words 'Love is stronger than death' (see Song 8:6) at the wedding of Prince Harry and Meghan Markle in 2018. In a remarkable demonstration of the power of direct preaching without a tight script, he quoted Martin Luther King Jr: 'We must discover the power of love, the redemptive power of love. And when we do that, we will make of this old world a new world, for love is the only way.'

Curry went on to press his point home: 'There's power in love. Don't underestimate it. Don't even over-sentimentalize it. There's power, power in love.'

The problem with love

It was a deeply moving sermon,[1] and the commentaries that wax lyrical about the power of love are equally inspiring. But as I heard the one and read the other, I found myself unconvinced. There's a problem if we just stop there with a lovely reassurance about the power of love. The problem is called death.

The Song of Songs deals with this. In chapter 8 we find a touching picture of the two lovers we have been tracking for so long:

Who is this coming up from the wilderness
    leaning on her beloved?
(Song 8:5a)

Mention of the wilderness takes us back to the exodus that took the people of Israel from misery and slavery in Egypt, through the rigours of the desert, into the Promised Land, a place of safety, flowing with milk and honey. We are lifted beyond the merely human to think of Christ leading us out of the misery of our sin, through the wilderness of this life, to our own promised land, the new creation. But we must not miss one touching detail. The woman is *leaning* on her beloved. When do people lean on each other? Usually when they are weak, ill, incapacitated or *old*.

Taking the last of these possibilities, is it too speculative to see this as the couple in old age? If this is the case, the verses that follow express their reflections on their lives together, forming the climax of the book. The woman looks back to the early days of the relationship, and indeed of her lover's life:

> Under the apple tree I roused you;
>> there your mother conceived you,
>> there she who was in labour gave you birth.
> (Song 8:5b)

This reminds her of all they have had together through so many years, and moves her to ask for even more closeness:

> Place me like a seal over your heart,
>> like a seal on your arm . . .
> (Song 8:6)

Sealed for good

It is a simple picture of total and unbreakable intimacy. She wants to be at his heart, the centre of his being, and on his arm where it is public. She speaks with both urgency and confidence about this because of what she now understands of the nature of love.

Like death, love grabs hold of you and won't let go. This is what happens in courtship and grows through marriage: 'its jealousy unyielding as the grave' (8:6).

The woman pictures a grave as a jealous person who will not let go. Death is like that. So is love, she says.

Tremper Longman describes the power of jealousy:

Humans can have only one God. If they worship another, it triggers God's jealousy. God's jealousy is an energy that tries to rescue the relationship. Similarly, a man and a woman can have only one spouse. If there is a threat to that relationship, then jealousy is a proper emotion. All this is because so much hangs on the integrity of the relationship. It is so basic, so deep, that it stirs up strong emotions and passions.[2]

Love indestructible?

Fire is another way of expressing the power of love, because flames consume everything that stands in their way:

It burns like blazing fire,
　like a mighty flame.
(Song 8:6b)

Love rages and blazes like a forest fire that cannot be contained. Yet another comparison is the power of water:

Many waters cannot quench love;
　rivers cannot sweep it away.
(Song 8:7a)

The woman claims something even greater – that love is indestructible. In the Old Testament, water, particularly the sea, represents the forces of chaos, just the kind of thing we fear will strike us. However, they cannot touch love, she says. But is she right?

Human love cannot overcome death because all relationships and marriages will ultimately end in death (if nothing else). It's not for no reason that in the marriage vows couples say, 'Until death do us part.' That means that even at the beginning of a marriage the anticipation of its ending is foregrounded.

I hate to sound crass, but it's easy to say, 'Many waters cannot quench love. Rivers cannot sweep it away.' But what happens when a woman's husband is drowned? Surely the text itself invites a closer look. In the end, the jealousy of the grave is stronger than the jealousy of love, isn't it?

Death hovers

The wrenching truth of life in a fallen world is that death is inevitable. Clever commentators study the Song's words about the indestructibility of love and try to find ways of making them meaningful. They speak of how the very fact of writing them and recording the relationship in the Song confers a sort of immortality. It's a lovely thought.

You will find something similar in a poem by Philip Larkin, 'An Arundel Tomb'. He writes about seeing a stone tomb in a church in Sussex. On the top are stone effigies of the earl and the countess buried there. The distinctive features of their faces have been gradually worn away so that their individuality has been lost. But one special feature has defied the centuries. The stonemason carved them holding hands. This sparks off something in Larkin, who finishes his poem by asserting that after we die the one thing that remains is love.[3]

Clutching at straws

Larkin's thought is very beautiful, but the more closely you examine it, the flimsier a comfort it is for either married or single people, let alone someone who has been widowed.

I went to the funeral of a neighbour. It was warm, affectionate and dignified. For whatever reason, the person who gave the address didn't feel that it was right to talk about the Christian gospel. What people heard was in many ways a kind attempt to say something to people who weren't Christians about the ongoing 'whatever' of the lady who had died; to say that she lived on in us; her memory lived with us; we had memories of her. And so those memories were how she lived on. It was beautifully done but an absolute and total failure – because how can a memory compare with a person?

Raging against the dying of the light

How much better to rage against the horrors of death, which, humanly speaking, *is* stronger than love in that it brings every relationship to some sort of end. That is what Brandon Flowers, lead singer of The Killers, does in a powerful song called 'A Dustland Fairytale' about his parents' courtship in the early 1960s and his mother's early death from cancer. As he tells the story, even in the early days he says the devil was lying in wait. Whether the 'devil' here is cancer or Satan who includes cancer in his armoury, it is stronger than love and it takes away his family's happiness: the castles in the sky of their dreams are left vandalized. The singer is left to mourn and protest at the cruelty of life, where the good die young.[4]

Is that what we have to choose between? Settling for living on in people's memories or raging against a cruel universe? No. There is a fuller meaning to this text, in Christ.

A power greater than death

We find in Jesus Christ the power of a love that is not just like the power of death but also breaks the power of death. The power of a love that is not just like the jealousy of the grave but smashes the jealousy of the grave. The power of a love which is like fire and which many waters cannot overcome because that fire will burn beyond death in the lives of those who have received it. In fact the whole of this life is simply a preparation for what will follow beyond death.

Something better

If we are too wrapped up in the loves and delights of romance and marriage and family in this world, we need to be reminded that one day these will come to an end and that actually there is something they point to that is even better. The incompleteness of our experience of love in this life points to something greater and better, for us now and for ever. This is the love of Jesus Christ, which took him into the holocaust of the cross, where as a burnt offering he gave himself for our sin and then triumphed over the grave.

The fiercest jealousy of that tomb longed to hold on to him. How much Satan wanted to keep the body of the Son of God in that tomb but could not! This is the love that the chaos of death could not break. This is where we truly experience 'friendship caught on fire'.[5]

Iain Duguid discusses this idea further:

> In Jesus we truly experience friendship on fire . . . God's friendship on fire pursues us right where we are with all our lostness, brokenness and coldness, with all our failures to love him and others, and all our sins both outside and within marriage.[6]

He loves you with a love so strong that it is like the power of death in the way that it grabs hold of you. But he's even greater than the power of death.

God loves you with the living flame of love, and he's always moving towards you so that it can burn more in your soul and replicate the same love within you. It is the flame of divine love that will take us through death to the other side, into the new creation.

That's what our delving into the Song of Songs has been about. As Dane Ortlund says: 'The Christian life is not an ascetic life, but a life in which every received pleasure draws the mind up to supreme Pleasure, Christ himself, in his resplendent beauty. Joy is fundamentally a vision of God.'[7]

There have been some useful insights into marital and romantic and human love, I hope, that have inspired and helped us. But all the way through we've been thinking about how this teaches us too about Christ's love for his church, and how that is greater. Even the best human love is not an end in itself, but a pointer towards Christ. We cycle and circle and spiral around it in this life, until we meet it perfectly in the next.

The great hymnwriter Isaac Watts (1674–1748) expressed this truth beautifully:

From thee, my God, my joys shall rise,
And run eternal rounds,
Beyond the limits of the skies,
And all created bounds.

The holy triumphs of my soul
Shall death itself outbrave,
Leave dull mortality behind,
And fly beyond the grave.

There, where my blessed Jesus reigns,
In heav'n's unmeasured space,
I'll spend a long eternity
In pleasure and in praise.

Millions of years my wond'ring eyes
Shall o'er thy beauties rove,
And endless ages I'll adore
The glories of thy love.

Sweet Jesus, every smile of thine
Shall fresh endearments bring;
And thousand tastes of new delight
From all thy graces spring.

Haste, my Beloved, fetch my soul
Up to thy blest abode;
Fly, for my spirit longs to see
My Saviour and my God.[8]

Questions

- How does the fear of death affect your attitude to those you love?
- How does the gospel help us with this?

Prayer

Lord, I thank you that whatever else death may take away from me, you will never be taken away. Amen.

Conclusion:
The power of spiritual marriage in the storms of life

I hope I have managed to show you convincingly that Jesus is the Lover of your soul, and how this can be a felt experience in your life.

I want to finish by giving you a sense of how important this can be. It would be easy to dismiss what we have been writing about as a rather rarified and ethereal topic, of interest to the more dreamy, mystically minded type of Christian but of limited practical relevance to most of us.

I'm reminded of a passage from another Don Winslow novel: 'Jacqui leans back against the van wall and looks at Travis, who just finished shooting up himself. They smile at each other and then she drifts off into heroin world, so vastly superior to the real world.'[1]

Is that all it is? Spiritual escapism in which we leave normal life with all its trials and retreat to a pleasant but rather unreal place, like a kind of spiritual drug?

I want to tell you about some Christians who found that knowing Jesus as their Lover was a spiritual lifesaver in the storms of life.

Our ancestors – what kept them going?

In seventeenth-century England the early Baptists, Presbyterians and Congregationalists were subjected to severe persecution. More than two thousand of their ministers were ejected from their churches in 1662 because they would not accept the Anglican prayer book and Articles of Faith, as well as the king as the head of the church. It became illegal for them to preach.

What sustained these thousands of believers as they were facing this oppression from church and state authorities?

A remarkable piece of research by Elizabeth Clarke has shown that one of the central thoughts that helped them was in fact the personal, lover-like passion of Christ – what they called the 'spiritual marriage' – specifically for each of them as an individual believer, loved with all of the madness in Christ's soul. For them, it was a real-world faith-saver.[2]

Spiritual marriage

These free-church leaders turned (in the face of the loss of political influence, state recognition, even the legal right to preach and to meet for worship) to the theme of spiritual marriage as a way to bring them close individually to Christ as the Lover of their soul. One leader, James Janeway, published a book on the Song called *Heaven Upon Earth, or The Best Friend in the Worst of Times*, which spoke of the power of the experience of Christ described by the Song:

> Those that are acquainted with a spiritual life know these things ... that they are the greatest realities in the world ... They can tell you at such a time they were brought unto his Banquetting house and his Banner over them was Love: They can tell you at such a time Christ came into his Garden to eat his pleasant Fruits; at such a time they heard the voice of their Beloved, saying *Open to me, my Sister, my Spouse, my Love, my Dame, my Dove, my Undefiled.*[3]

Many of these ministers were imprisoned. Others had to meet secretly. Their political hopes were in tatters. Their family security had been destroyed. Their congregations were split or dispersed. They were marginalized and despised figures. Everything screamed mockingly at them, 'You've failed! You are a failure!'

They turned to the metaphor of spiritual marriage (as found especially in the Song) to be assured of the reality of Christ in their lives as they sought closer intimacy with him in the secret places of their souls. There they met Christ. They remembered that they were united with him, irrevocably – that he was theirs, and they were his. As they remembered, they experienced more than memory: communion with Christ himself, the Lover of their souls, who delighted in the beauty he found in them, and touched them in tenderness and affection like the strongest and gentlest of lovers.

No richer match

As they found new strength and hope, they preached the same to their congregations, often meeting in secret in houses and barns and woods, risking fines and imprisonment. Of course, they preached on a wide variety of biblical books and themes. But Clarke suggests that the influence of the Song of Songs was strong. Its imagery 'extended to that of contemporary romance as the preacher becomes a kind of marriage broker between Christ and the individual believer: "Do you ever expect a better offer? Can you hope for a better, a richer match?"'[4]

A powerful picture

The example of the early free-church leaders shows that the metaphor of spiritual marriage with Christ (as seen all through Scripture, including the Song of Songs) has a peculiar power for a Christian when life seems to be falling apart.

In the contemporary West many Christians feel marginalized and disempowered in a culture that is moving away from its Christian roots and increasingly seeing them as suspect. Often we are patronized, sometimes even scorned. It is a far less severe situation compared to that of Christians in many parts of the world today, and much less difficult than that of those early Nonconformists in seventeenth-century England. But, subjectively, it seems to us that we are in dark, stormy weather. When we feel like this, the metaphor of spiritual marriage with Christ has so much to offer us:

- the assurance of a love that will not let us go, as firm a commitment as wedding vows – even death will not part us from this Lover;
- the movement towards us of a Lover who meets us in a secret place that cannot be taken away from us;
- at the deepest depth of our souls, safety: our 'inner self is being securely held';[5]
- tender caresses of love and sweet spiritual sustenance;
- one who will take us back again and again when we are unfaithful to him;
- the promise of protection and security;
- the delight of Christ himself in what he is doing in us, even when others seem to point out our faults and we find ourselves agreeing with them;
- a foretaste of an ultimate wedding feast and the rock-solid guarantee of its eventual coming.

He *is* close

It matters that Jesus is near to us. We may often feel, like The Killers in their song 'Somebody Told Me', that heaven isn't close in this world.'[6] It's a common thing – the remoteness of heaven, the loneliness and pain of my existence. The experience of spiritual marriage brings heaven close, even in 'a place like this'. In the deep secret places of the soul, Christ himself draws near in gentleness and reassurance.

There is a private, walled garden which is his alone. Nothing need spoil our meeting with him there. It is a place kept for him, for his delight and ours with him. There we can know and feel his delight in us; we can find fresh joy in the sheer beauty of his person and the sweetness of his salvation – and, as those seventeenth-century Christians found, nothing can take that away.

Spurgeon rejoiced in the thought of that garden: 'Enclosed from the waste, walled around by grace, planted by instruction, visited by love, weeded by heavenly discipline, and guarded by divine power, one's favoured soul is prepared to yield fruit unto the Lord.'[7]

Calm amid the storm

Jonathan Edwards showed that he had such an experience of Christ when his church turned on him:

In the series of church meetings in 1750 at which he was rejected by his church by a vote of 230 to 23, one eyewitness, a pastor named David Hall, remarked: 'I never saw the least symptoms of displeasure in his countenance the whole week, but he appeared like a man of God, whose happiness was out of the reach of his enemies, and whose treasure was not only a future but a present good, overbalancing all imaginable ills of life.' Hall says this calmness on Edwards's part was 'to the astonishment of' those who opposed him.[8]

It's yours too

What was true for Jonathan Edwards can be true for you too. It really can. For your beloved Christ is yours, and you are his, and he grazes among the lilies. I rejoice in my dear wife Debbie and the thirty years we have been married, but I know that the best things about her point me to Christ, and I am sure she would say the same about me. Human love is incomplete and impermanent, but Jesus is ours for ever.

Charles Wesley sums it up in the words of his immortal hymn:

Jesus, Lover of my soul,
let me to thy bosom[9] fly,
while the nearer waters roll,
while the tempest still is high;
hide me, O my Saviour, hide,
till the storm of life is past;
safe into the haven guide,
O receive my soul at last!

Other refuge have I none;
hangs my helpless soul on thee;

leave, ah! leave me not alone,
still support and comfort me.
All my trust on thee is stayed,
all my help from thee I bring;
cover my defenceless head
with the shadow of thy wing.

Plenteous grace with thee is found,
grace to cover all my sin;
let the healing streams abound;
make and keep me pure within.
Thou of life the fountain art;
freely let me take of thee;
spring thou up within my heart,
rise to all eternity.[10]

Notes

1 Show me your face

1 *Christian Hymns* (Bridgend: Evangelical Movement of Wales, 1977), no. 619, author unknown (but possibly Charles Spurgeon). You can hear it online sung by a member of my church at: <https://youtu.be/0NGGiW81JXI>.

2 Dane C. Ortlund, *Edwards on the Christian Life: Alive to the beauty of God* (Wheaton, IL: Crossway, 2014), Kindle edn, loc. 29.

3 See: <https://phrases.org.uk/meanings/warts-and-all.html>, accessed 6 August 2019.

4 Ed Sheeran, 'Supermarket Flowers', *Divide*, Asylum/Atlantic Records, 2017.

5 Ortlund, *Edwards*, loc. 3968.

6 Alexander Ryrie, *Prayer of the Heart: An approach to silent prayer* (Oxford: SLG Press, 2017), p. 3.

7 Alafair Burke, *The Better Sister* (London: Faber & Faber, 2019), Kindle edn, loc. 1438.

8 The Killers, 'Sam's Town', *Sam's Town*, Island Records, 2006.

2 A supremely satisfying intimacy

1 Kari Jobe, 'Jesus, Lover of My Soul', *Kari Jobe*, Sparrow Records, 2009.

2 Charles Wesley (1707–88), 'Jesus, Lover of My Soul', in John and Charles Wesley, *Hymns and Sacred Poems* (London, 1740), pp. 67–68. Public domain.

3 Bruce Springsteen, 'Born to Run', *Born to Run*, Columbia Records, 1975.

4 I've borrowed the phrase 'crazy love' from Iain M. Duguid, *Song of Songs*, Reformed Expository Commentary (Phillipsburg, NJ: P&R, 2016), pp. 26–27.

5 See Song 1:2.

6 My favourite is Peter Lewis, *The Lord's Prayer: The greatest prayer in the world* (Milton Keynes: Paternoster, 2008).

3 Desire: you're the one that I want!

1 Opus 130.

2 I will try to demonstrate this in chapter 5.

3 Meatloaf, 'You Took the Words Right Out of My Mouth (Hot Summer Night)', *Bat Out of Hell*, Cleveland International / Epic Records, 1977.

4 Eugene H. Peterson, *Reversed Thunder: The Revelation of John and the praying imagination* (New York, NY: HarperOne, 1988), p. 147.

5 Iain M. Duguid, *Song of Songs*, Reformed Expository Commentary (Phillipsburg, NJ: P&R, 2016), p. 8.

4 Jesus is the Lover of my soul . . .

1 Tim Hughes, 'Beautiful One', *When Silence Falls*, Survivor Records, 2004.

2 Eugene H. Peterson, *Reversed Thunder: The Revelation of John and the praying imagination* (New York, NY: HarperOne, 1988), p. 156.

3 See Raymond C. Ortlund Jr, *God's Unfaithful Wife: A biblical theology of spiritual adultery*, New Studies in Biblical Theology (Downers Grove, IL: IVP, 1996). Ortlund provides lucid analysis.

4 Geoffrey Bromiley, quoted in John Piper, 'A metaphor of Christ and the church', *The Standard* 74(2) (February 1984). (Also available online at: <https://desiringgod.org/articles/a-metaphor-of-christ-and-the-church>, accessed 27 August 2019.)

5 Raymond C. Ortlund Jr, *Marriage and the Mystery of the Gospel* (Wheaton, IL: Crossway, 2016), p. 16.

6 So subtle that I would have completely missed it without the help of Ray Ortlund in *God's Unfaithful Wife*, pp. 143ff.

7 Ortlund, *God's Unfaithful Wife*, pp. 143ff.

8 Ortlund, *God's Unfaithful Wife*, pp. 143ff.

9 Richard Sibbes, 'Bowels opened, or expository sermons on Canticles IV. 16. V. V1', in *Works of Richard Sibbes*, ed. Alexander B. Grosart, 7 vols. (Edinburgh: James Nichol, 1862; repr. Banner of Truth, 2001), vol. 2, p. 7.

10 Charles Spurgeon, 'The Lord's own view of his church and people', *The Metropolitan Tabernacle Pulpit*, sermon no. 1957, Spurgeon Gems: <https://spurgeongems.org/vols31-33/chs1957.pdf>, accessed 5 August 2019.

5 Us: how the Song of Songs is about Jesus and me

1 Tyndale House, Cambridge, a marvellous community and a rich set of resources. The staff even let unscholarly and non-academic local pastors like me in to join the fun.

2 In Hebrew!

3 In Song 8:6 'fire, like a mighty flame' could be translated 'fire, like the very flame of the LORD'.

4 The emphasis is mine.

5 Reaching only the start of chapter 3 – they are rich reading. See Bernard of Clairvaux, *Sermons on the Song of Songs*, tr. Kilian Walsh and Irene M. Edmonds, 4 vols., Cistercian Fathers 40 (Kalamazoo, MI: Cistercian Publications, 1980).

6 It has been suggested that John Calvin was one of the early adopters of the merely human reading of the Song. However, if you look at the Bible references to the Song in Calvin's *Institutes of the Christian Religion* (1536), you find that two of the three use the spiritual reading of the text as though that were the right way to read it.

7 An example from Cambridge in 1990.

8 This connection to wisdom literature in the Bible is explored persuasively in the work of Dr Ros Clarke; see <http://rosclarke.co.uk/publications>.

9 Iain M. Duguid, *The Song of Songs: An introduction and commentary*, Tyndale Old Testament Commentaries 19 (Downers Grove, IL: IVP Academic, 2015), pp. 37–38.

10 Matthew Henry, *Commentary on the Whole Bible*, 6 vols. (London, 1706–21). Public domain. (The unabridged text is available at Christian Classics Ethereal Library: https://ccel.org/h/henry/mhc2/MHC00000.HTM, accessed 22 August 2020.)

6 Insecurity: will you still love me tomorrow?

1 Fear Of Missing Out, one of the pandemics of the age.

2 See: <https://instagram.com/p/BtRMUjKF-e7>, accessed 21 August 2020.

3 Alexandra Jones, 'I tried "Instagram face" for a week and here's what happened . . .', BBC News, 17 August 2018: <https://bbc.co.uk/bbcthree/article/5c237a34-7a47-4deb-a5b4-a23e77cc88f7>, accessed 2 August 2019.

4 I am grateful to Matt Lillicrap who explained this to me, and who pointed me to his own source, a sermon by Mark Driscoll on Song of Songs 1. I am not endorsing everything Driscoll has preached or written on the Song. But *this* point seems to me exceptionally insightful and helpful.

5 I have put both flower names in quotation marks because it is not absolutely clear which plant species are meant.

6 Don Winslow, *The Power of the Dog* (London: Arrow, 2006), p. 393.

7 Martin Luther, 'The freedom of a Christian' (1520), in *The Annotated Luther, vol. 1: The Roots of Reform*, ed. Timothy J. Wengert (Minneapolis, MN: Fortress Press, 2015), p. 104.

8 Owen Strachan and Doug Sweeney, *Jonathan Edwards on Beauty*, The Essential Edwards Collection (Chicago, IL: Moody Press, 2010), Kindle edn, loc. 1457.

9 Martyn Waites, *The Old Religion* (London: Bonnier Zaffre, 2018), Kindle edn, loc. 3285.

10 The Killers, 'Sam's Town', *Sam's Town*, Island Records, 2006.

11 Thanks to the friend, who remains anonymous!

12 I have used the NRSV here because 'my love' is a bit easier for men in particular to read than 'my darling', and the 'Ah's represent something in what the lover says that it does us good to hear.

7 Delight: the power of beauty

1 Again I have quoted the NRSV here because it retains the word 'beautiful' for her description of him, and I like the translation 'Ah'.

2 Dane C. Ortlund, *Edwards on the Christian Life: Alive to the beauty of God* (Wheaton, IL: Crossway, 2014), Kindle edn, loc. 319.

3 Ortlund, *Edwards*, loc. 154.

4 *The Works of John Owen*, ed. William H. Goold, 16 vols. (Edinburgh: Banner of Truth Trust, 1965), vol. 2, pp. 77–78.

5 William Blake, *The Marriage of Heaven and Hell* (1783), line 92: <https://www.bartleby.com/235/253.html>. Public domain.

6 Philip Ryken, *The Love of Loves in the Song of Songs* (Wheaton, IL: Crossway, 2019), p. 57.

7 All emphasis in these Scripture quotations is mine.

8 I owe this thought to Tim Chester.

8 Springtime: when fancy turns to love

1 This was your author and his wife-to-be.

2 I have substituted the word 'broken' for 'contrite' which is what you will find in just about every English translation since the King James Version in 1611. Unfortunately, modern translators appear not to have noticed that the English word 'contrite' meant something different in the early seventeenth century – 'broken, smashed, pulverized, ground up' – from what it has come to mean today – 'sorry, remorseful' – and that earlier meaning is what the Hebrew word means too! Thanks to Pete Williams of Tyndale House for confirming this analysis of both the English and Hebrew words.

3 I owe this insight to one of Bernard of Clairvaux's sermons on this text.

4 Dane C. Ortlund, *Edwards on the Christian Life: Alive to the beauty of God* (Wheaton, IL: Crossway, 2014), Kindle edn, loc. 738.

5 Ortlund, *Edwards*, loc. 731.

6 The Beatles, 'Here Comes the Sun', *Abbey Road*, Apple Records, 1969.

7 T. S. Eliot, 'The Waste Land' (1922), *The Complete Poems and Plays* (London: Faber & Faber, 2004), p. 59.

8 Florence and the Machine, 'South London Forever', *High as Hope*, Republic and Virgin EMI Records, 2018.

9 *Works of Richard Sibbes*, ed. Alexander B. Grosart, 7 vols. (Edinburgh: Banner of Truth Trust, 1983), vol. 2, p. 29.

10 Robert W. Jenson, *Song of Songs*, Interpretation: A Bible Commentary for Teaching and Preaching (Louisville, KY: Westminster John Knox Press, 2005), p. 35.

9 Belonging: together, for ever

1 Charles Spurgeon, 'The church's love to her loving Lord', *The Metropolitan Tabernacle Pulpit*, sermon no. 636, Spurgeon Gems: <http://spurgeongems.org/vols10-12/chs636.pdf>, accessed 5 August 2019.

2 Katie Roiphe, 'Liberated in love: can open marriage work?', *Harper's Bazaar*, 13 July 2019: <https://harpersbazaar.com/culture/features/a400/open-marriages-0809>, accessed 2 August 2019.

3 Gabrielle Donnelly, 'Life on planet Tilda', *Daily Mail*, 16 March 2014: <https://dailymail.co.uk/tvshowbiz/article-2581905/Life-planet-Tilda-No-TV-Wearing-sons-clothes-Why-partner-ex-really-good-friends-unflattering-view-England.html>, accessed 2 August 2019.

4 I owe this observation to Pete Williams in private correspondence.

5 Ellen F. Davis, *Proverbs, Ecclesiastes, and the Song of Songs*, Westminster Bible Companion (Louisville, KY: Westminster John Knox Press, 2000), p. 295.

6 Carole King, singing her own version of the song on the *Tapestry* album (Ode Records, 1971), and in a marvellous live version from a BBC2 session available online, picks up the vulnerability of the young woman better than anyone.

7 William Cowper, 'Hark, My Soul, It Is the Lord' (1768), *The Complete Poetical Works of William Cowper* (Edinburgh: Gail & Inglis, 1853), pp. 243–244. Public domain. (Also available online at: <https://poemhunter.com/poem/lovest-thou-me>, accessed 20 August 2020.)

10 Distance: we've lost that loving feeling

1 Nicely described in Peter Lewis, *The Genius of Puritanism* (Grand Rapids, MI: Reformation Heritage, 2008).

2 More on this in chapter 15.

3 Zack Eswine, *Spurgeon's Sorrows: Realistic hope for those who suffer from depression* (Fearn: Christian Focus, 2015), Kindle edn, loc. 509.

4 Eswine, *Spurgeon's Sorrows*, loc. 912.

5 Bob Dylan, 'Every Grain of Sand', *Shot of Love*, Columbia Records, 1981.

6 Iain M. Duguid, *Song of Songs*, Reformed Expository Commentary (Phillipsburg, NJ: P&R, 2016), p. 63.

7 Eswine, *Spurgeon's Sorrows*, loc. 1850.

11 Christ finds us beautiful

1 Song 1:15–16 NRSV.

2 All emphasis in these Scripture quotations is mine.

3 In Isaiah 61:3 the word translated in the NIV as 'beauty' in the phrase 'crown of beauty' is the same in Hebrew as the word translated 'splendour' in 'for the display of his splendour' at the end of the verse.

4 Quoted in Dane C. Ortlund, *Edwards on the Christian Life: Alive to the beauty of God* (Wheaton, IL: Crossway, 2014), Kindle edn, loc. 410.

5 James Durham, *Clavis Cantici, or An Exposition of the Song of Solomon* (Aberdeen: George King, 1840), p. 117.

6 Matthew Henry on Song of Songs 1:15, *Commentary on the Whole Bible*, 6 vols. (1706–21), vol. 3. Public domain.

7 Charles Spurgeon, 'Christ's estimate of his people', *The New Park Street Pulpit*, sermon no. 282, Spurgeon's Gems: <https://spurgeongems.org/vols4-6/chs282.pdf>, accessed 5 August 2019.

8 Spurgeon, 'Christ's estimate of his people': <https://spurgeongems.org/sermon/chs282.pdf>, accessed 22 August 2020.

9 Ortlund, *Edwards*, loc. 441.

12 Christ gets crazy with love

1 In Iain Duguid's apt phrase. See *Song of Songs*, Reformed Expository Commentary (Phillipsburg, NJ: P&R, 2016), pp. 26–27.

2 Alexander Pope, *The Rape of the Lock* (1714), Canto II, lines 27–28: <https://bartleby.com/203/42.html>. Public domain.

3 See Glynn Harrison's important book of this title: *A Better Story: God, sex and human flourishing* (London: IVP, 2017).

4 See also Tim Chester's equally important book (on pornography): *Captured by a Better Vision: Living porn-free* (Nottingham: IVP, 2010).

5 Daniel C. Fredericks and Daniel J. Estes, *Ecclesiastes and the Song of Songs*, Apollos Old Testament Commentary (Nottingham: Apollos, 2010), p. 363.

6 As is the question of what we do when we are not in a position to give this particular gift. (We will return to this.)

7 Charles Spurgeon, 'Christ's estimate of his people', *The New Park Street Pulpit*, sermon no. 282, Spurgeon's Gems: <https://spurgeongems.org/vols4-6/chs282.pdf>, accessed 5 August 2019.

13 Finally, the wedding!

1 A real-life example.

2 Amelia and Greg Clarke, *One Flesh: A practical guide to honeymoon sex and beyond* (Sydney: Matthias Media, 2013) is detailed, practical and wise in this sensitive area.

3 *The Works of John Owen*, ed. William H. Goold, 16 vols. (Edinburgh: Banner of Truth Trust, 1965), vol. 2, p. 118.

4 Peter Masters, *The Mutual Love of Christ and His People: An explanation of the Song of Solomon for personal devotions and Bible study groups* (London: The Wakeman Trust, 2004), p. 75.

5 'A Spiritual Canticle of the Soul and the Bridegroom Christ', 36:5, *The Complete Works of Saint John of the Cross, Doctor of the Church*, tr. E. Allison Peers (London: Burns Oates, 1943), vol. 2, pp. 380–381.

14 Not tonight, dear!

1 I have no idea who these people are!

2 Justin Whitmel Earley, *The Common Rule: Habits of purpose for an age of distraction* (Downers Grove, IL: IVP, 2019), pp. 79ff. This book is full of practical helps for ordering our lives so that we can know more of Christ.

3 William Cowper, 'Seeking the Beloved', *The Complete Poetical Works of William Cowper* (Edinburgh: Gail & Inglis, 1853), pp. 251–253. Public domain. (Also available online at: <https://poemhunter.com/poem/seeking-the-beloved>, accessed 7 August 2019.)

15 Spiritual intimacy betrayed and lost through porn

1 From the leaflet *Open Eyes and Free Lives* (Salford: Naked Truth Project, 2019).

2 The question of the morality of masturbation for Christians is hotly debated. While there is no single biblical command against it, the overall pattern of biblical teaching about sex and sexual sin means that the onus is on the individual to be really sure before God that masturbating does not violate his will, particularly when there are mental image and fantasies that accompany it. See the balanced discussion in Wayne Grudem, *Christian Ethics: An introduction to biblical moral reasoning* (Wheaton, IL: Crossway, 2018), pp. 724–728.

3 The Specials, 'Too Much Too Young', *The Specials*, 2-Tone Records, 1979.

4 Wendy Maltz and Larry Maltz, *The Porn Trap: The essential guide to overcoming problems caused by pornography* (New York, NY: HarperCollins, 2008), p. 13.

5 Maltz and Maltz, *The Porn Trap*, p. 72.

6 Maltz and Maltz, *The Porn Trap*, p. 265.

7 Maltz and Maltz, *The Porn Trap*, p. 265.

8 Maltz and Maltz, *The Porn Trap*, p. 24.

9 Maltz and Maltz, *The Porn Trap*, p. 148.

10 'Ex-porn addict reveals how the habit destroyed her heart', The Christian Institute, 6 May 2014: <https://christian.org.uk/news/ex-porn-addict-reveals-how-the-habit-destroyed-her-heart>, accessed 22 August 2019.

11 Evidence for this is provided in Gail Dines, *Pornland: How porn has hijacked our sexuality* (Boston, MA: Beacon Press, 2011).

12 Maltz and Maltz, *The Porn Trap*, p. 219.

13 See Paula Hall, *Sex Addiction: The partner's perspective* (London: Routledge, 2015).

14 Sex inside marriage can also be idolatrous like this.

15 One of the leading Christian experts on porn addiction, Paula Hall, sees three main entry gates to porn use: (1) some sort of issue with feeling securely attached to the love of a parent or significant other as a child; (2) some sort of psychological trauma; (3) simply being exposed to porn and being reeled in by it. In every case, some sort of exposure/opportunity is of course necessary. Hall's professional (and secular) organization reports that for an increasing number of porn addicts, it is simply exposure. That matches my pastoral work

with men from strong Christian family backgrounds. See Paula Hall, *Confronting Porn* (Salford: Naked Truth Resources, 2016), ch. 5.

16 See Genesis 25:29–34.

17 The only qualification I would make to this blanket statement is that a sense of sexual attraction is part of how we assess whether we are going to marry someone. We see this in the early chapters of the Song. While it would be inhuman and unbiblical to repress this completely, like a butterfly being squashed under a boot, it does need very careful control, like descending a very steep hill on a bike with the brakes on so as to keep to the speed limit and not fly off at the corner, however exhilarating it might feel to let go and let gravity take over.

16 Porn-spoiled lives restored by Christ

1 Led Zeppelin, 'Heartbreaker', *Led Zeppelin II*, Atlantic Records, 1969.

2 Ray Ortlund, 'Virginity restored', The Gospel Coalition, 15 August 2008: <https://thegospelcoalition.org/blogs/ray-ortlund/virginity-restored>, accessed 22 August 2019.

3 Ortlund, 'Virginity restored'.

4 Daniel C. Fredericks and Daniel J. Estes, *Ecclesiastes and the Song of Songs*, Apollos Old Testament Commentary (Nottingham: Apollos, 2010), p. 363.

5 Wendy Maltz and Larry Maltz, *The Porn Trap: The essential guide to overcoming problems caused by pornography* (New York, NY: HarperCollins, 2008), p. 159.

6 Maltz and Maltz, *The Porn Trap*, p. 161.

7 Jenni Russell, 'Pursuit of perfection is what makes us sad: we need to develop emotional intelligence and accept our flaws to survive in the modern world', *The Times*, 8 August 2019: <https://thetimes.co.uk/article/pursuit-of-perfection-is-what-makes-us-sad-6z5rtbcg9>.

8 Maltz and Maltz, *The Porn Trap*, p. 258.

9 Maltz and Maltz, *The Porn Trap*, p. 259.

17 Reconciliation: back together again

1 Gary Brady, *Song of Solomon: Heavenly love*, Welwyn Commentary Series (Darlington / Webster, NY: Evangelical Press, 2006), pp. 186–187.

2 *Banner of Truth* magazine, April 2007, p. 1.

18 Still beautiful after all these years

1 John Piper, *The Pleasures of God: Meditations in God's delight in being God*, rev. edn (Fearn: Christian Focus, 2013).

2 Charles Spurgeon, 'Overcoming Christ', *The Metropolitan Tabernacle Pulpit*, sermon no. 2486, Spurgeon Gems: <http:// spurgeongems.org/vols40-42/chs2486.pdf>, accessed 6 August 2019.

3 Martin Luther, *Luther's Works, vol. 12: Selected Psalms I*, ed. Jaroslav Pelikan, Hilton C. Oswald and Helmut T. Lehmann (St Louis, MO: Concordia, 1999), p. 279.

4 Luther, *Selected Psalms I*, p. 279.

5 Martin Luther, 'The freedom of a Christian' (1520), in *The Annotated Luther, vol. 1: The Roots of Reform*, ed. Timothy J. Wengert (Minneapolis, MN: Fortress Press, 2015), pp. 499–501.

6 Dane C. Ortlund, *Edwards on the Christian Life: Alive to the beauty of God* (Wheaton, IL: Crossway, 2014), Kindle edn, loc. 429.

7 Ortlund, *Edwards*, loc. 416.

8 Duncan Hamilton, *For the Glory: The life of Eric Liddell* (London: Transworld, 2016), Kindle edn, loc. 4595.

9 Radiohead, 'Fake Plastic Trees', *The Bends*, Parlophone/Capitol Records, 1995.

19 The spiral staircase of longing and love

1 James Joyce, *Finnegans Wake* (London: Faber & Faber, 1939).

2 Richard S. Hess, *Song of Songs*, Baker Commentary on the Old Testament Wisdom and Psalms (Grand Rapids, MI: Baker Academic, 2005), p. 250, quoting Dianne Bergant, *The Song of Songs*, Berit Olam (Collegeville, MN: Liturgical Press, 2001), p. 105.

3 John Murray, *Redemption Accomplished and Applied* (Grand Rapids, MI: Eerdmans, 2015; originally published 1955), pp. 179–180.

4 Hess, *Song of Songs*, p. 227.

5 Ellen F. Davis, *Proverbs, Ecclesiastes, and the Song of Songs*, Westminster Bible Companion (Louisville, KY: Westminster John Knox Press, 2000), p. 302.

6 Davis, *Proverbs, Ecclesiastes, and the Song of Songs*, p. 302.

20 Love is stronger than death

1 However, for a critical analysis see John Stevens, 'Powerful preaching: what can we learn from the sermon of Bishop Michael Curry at the royal wedding?', John Stevens: Dissenting Opinion, 5 June 2018: <http://john-stevens.com/2018/06/powerful-preaching-what-can-we-learn.html>, accessed 10 March 2020.

2 Tremper Longman III, *Song of Songs*, New International Commentary on the Old Testament (Grand Rapids, MI: Eerdmans, 2001), pp. 211–212, quoted in Richard S. Hess, *Song of Songs*, Baker Commentary on the Old Testament Wisdom and Psalms (Grand Rapids, MI: Baker Academic, 2005), p. 239.

3 Philip Larkin, 'An Arundel Tomb' (1956), *The Whitsun Weddings* (London: Faber & Faber, 1964), p. 46.

4 The Killers, 'A Dustland Fairytale', *Day & Age*, Island Records, 2008.

5 As described, remarkably, by the actor Bruce Lee: 'Love is like a friendship caught on fire. In the beginning a flame, very pretty, often hot and fierce, but still only light and flickering. As love grows older, our hearts mature and our love becomes as coals, deep-burning and unquenchable.' Bruce Lee, *Artist of Life*, ed. John Little (Boston: Tuttle, 1999), p. 96, cited in Iain M. Duguid, *Song of Songs*, Reformed Expository Commentary (Phillipsburg, NJ: P&R, 2016), p. 138. I found this great phrase in Philip Ryken's exposition of the Song: *The Love of Loves in the Song of Songs* (Wheaton, IL: Crossway, 2019), p. 137.

6 Duguid, *Song of Songs*, p. 144.

7 Dane C. Ortlund, *Edwards on the Christian Life: Alive to the beauty of God* (Wheaton, IL: Crossway, 2014), Kindle edn, loc. 1511.

8 Isaac Watts, 'From Thee, My God, My Joys Shall Rise', *The Psalms and Hymns of Isaac Watts* (London, 1806), hymn 75. Public domain. (The complete book is available at Christian Classics Ethereal Library: http://ccel.org/ccel/watts/psalmshymns.html, accessed 22 August 2020.)

Conclusion: The power of spiritual marriage in the storms of life

1 Don Winslow, *The Border* (London: HarperCollins, 2020), Kindle edn, loc. 26762.

2 Elizabeth Clarke, *Politics, Religion and the Song of Songs in Seventeenth-Century England* (Basingstoke: Palgrave Macmillan, 2011).

3 Quoted in Clarke, *Politics, Religion and the Song of Songs*, p. 182.

4 James Janeway, quoted in Clarke, *Politics, Religion and the Song of Songs*, p. 182.

5 Alexander Ryrie, *Wonderful Exchange: An exploration of silent prayer* (Norwich: Canterbury Press), p. 58.

6 The Killers, 'Somebody Told Me', *Hot Fuss*, Island Records, 2004.

7 Charles Spurgeon, 'Plentiful refreshment', *Faith's Check Book*, Gospel Web, 24 September 2014: <http://gospelweb.net/SpurgeonDevotions/Spurgeon0829.htm>, accessed 8 September 2019.

8 Dane C. Ortlund, *Edwards on the Christian Life: Alive to the beauty of God* (Wheaton, IL: Crossway, 2014), Kindle edn, loc. 519.

9 Remember what we noted earlier – that the meaning of 'bosom' in English used to include a man's chest, as in the account of the Last Supper in the Authorized Version: 'Now there was leaning on Jesus' bosom one of his disciples, whom Jesus loved' (John 13:23 KJV).

10 Charles Wesley, 'Jesus, Lover of My Soul', in John and Charles Wesley, *Hymns and Sacred Poems* (London, 1740), pp. 67–68. Public domain.